Over 50 STARTING OVER ®

Max Gilreath   Deanna Poehlman

ADVANCED PRAISE FOR
Over 50 STARTING OVER ®

"If you have a chance to read anything Deanna has written, hear anything she has to say, to see anything that she does, I tell you this, that you need to take that to heart because she sees herself as a vessel, and while I give her credit for my success all the time, she gives it to our Creator, and she takes just pure joy in being the vessel to be used to bring that happiness to me."

Chad Pilbeam - Owner, Beer Logic

"Max shares lessons learned about the business world that have crazy value - pearls, tossed out for free. As Max steps into the story and progression of his life I begin to relate more and more to the "Beach ball Challenges and Issues". Deanna talks about grieving after job loss. This is really amazing. I have never really thought about it this way."

Mitch Kreigh - Retired Sr. Warrant Officer, United States Army

"This book is must read for professionals starting over due to changes in the economy, technology paradigm shifts, or just a desire to find more fulfillment in their vocation. I wish something like this had been available to me early in my career. It puts into words many of my own thoughts and feelings, and I now realize I wasn't the only one struggling to find my way through the maze. I applaud Max Gilreath for his real and personable story, how he battled his way to success and ultimately found peace with his career experiences and life in general."

Scott Collier - Retired Corporate Executive

"Just like in every story where the hero succeeds it is because of the guide they encountered that provided them the best plan of action. Max & Deanna are providing you with the perfect plan to help you realize your full potential and dreams as you are starting over. Max's book 'Over 50 Starting Over' helps you avoid the feelings of I'm alone and no one understands and what do I do now, by allowing you to walk through Max's journey and Deanna's guidance. It put into words what we have experienced and had not been able to express. Yes, ultimately it is up to us to find a plan and make it work, now Max & Deanna have provided the plan all you have to do is follow it. We also feel reading it with your spouse helps to open up some conversations you were avoiding or didn't realize you had not been discussing."

Roy & Gail Randolph - Owners, KartHost

Over 50 STARTING OVER ®

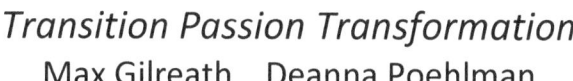

Transition Passion Transformation
Max Gilreath   Deanna Poehlman

Copyright © 2016 by Over 50 Starting Over

ISBN - 13   978-0-692-86692-4
ISBN - 10   0692866922

All rights reserved. No part of this book may be reproduced or transmitted in any form or by any means, electronic or mechanical, including photocopying and recording, or by any information storage and retrieval system, without permission in writing from the publisher.

Unless otherwise noted, Scripture is taken from The New Living Translation (NLT), copyright 1996, 2004 by Tyndale House Publishers, Inc.

Printed in the United States of America

First printing, 2017

Publicist: Debbie Christa-Ortiz
Editor: Robin Sweet
Illustrator: David Bishop Bamberg
Book cover: James Cook
Furniture design on cover: Cantoni, Houston

www.over50startingover.net

Contents

Chapter One
    A Bigger Life..... Sink or Swim   1

Chapter Two
    "Something Special"..... Markers That Color Life   21

Chapter Three
    Behaviors and Influences..... We Know-It-All Years   42

Chapter Four
    Keep Moving Forward.....Clear But Not   56

Chapter Five
    Career and Cronyism....."Smoke Screen"   70

Chapter Six
    Gain, Loss, Gain.....WTH Happened   90

Chapter Seven
    Real Change.....Starting to Get It   114

Chapter Eight
    Awakening Within.....Integral Design   131

Chapter Nine
    Midlife Crisis.....Loss of Real Identity   151

Chapter Ten
    Give Yourself Permission.....You're in Control   164

Chapter Eleven
    Completely Alive.....Endless Possibilities   185

Chapter Twelve
    From Caterpillar to Butterfly... Living It Every Day   209

Dedications

This book is dedicated to my deceased family members; brothers, "Chip", and James, Uncle Ken, and my parents, Margaret and Dwight Gilreath. Your love, inspiration, care and memories helped shape my life's identity. To my sons, daughter and granddaughters, your love is all that I need. To family and friends, your contributions and teachings are part of my being. To the people of the world, who feel unworthy or unsure of living a life of passion, purpose and meaning, believe that you can and you will. *Max*

With much honor I dedicate this book in love to my husband, Bob, who has always supported my character, and untamed passion for doing what I love. Each day begins and ends with my appreciation to our Creator for your love and friendship and the fact that I get to share life with my most favorite person. God's most valued gift to me is the privilege of being your wife and enjoying the last 30 years and next many more being your best cheerleader. Thank you for sticking with me through all of our 'Starting Over's from life's transitions' and always having enough grace in your grace tank to sustain us through them all. I love you. *Your Bride, Deanna*

Acknowledgements

From the book's inception, step-by-step, every person, resource, and instruction needed to construct and develop every aspect of the book was found in people that we had already developed trusting relationships with. Everything and everyone, from advisors, to branding team, to our web and social media platforms, were systematically conveniently positioned and made available.

We are grateful to a wonderful team of professionals - their dedication and contributions made this book possible. Many thanks to Deanna Poehlman, co-author, business partner and friend, for her enormous contributions and belief in this book, and in me. Her coaching and counseling have made an immeasurable difference in my life.

We are indebted to our talented and dedicated, project development team, suppliers, and vendor partners who have worked so diligently to support our efforts, believing in the mission and goals for the book. I have met so many open, gracious, and hospitable midlifers, and seniors over the years, many of whom have shared time, wisdom, and experience with me and have contributed to this book.

Deanna and I have to extend the greatest of gratitude to two vital contributors. First, our business partner, great friend, marketing extraordinaire and publishing connoisseur Debbie Christa-Ortiz. Deanna says if we were a bowling team, Debbie would be our anchor man. She keeps us on task, grounded, and no one extended more expertise and God-given talent for writing and going to market with this book than Her. So, Debbie, please know how much you are truly appreciated!

Second, to our beloved editor, Robin Sweet. Robin has the biggest grace tank of the team and her expertise and precision in the editing process has awed us all. Robin, please know how much you are greatly valued and how truly thankful and blessed we are to have you work on this project with us. In addition, we thank you for your friendship.

To my former wife and mother of my sons - you are a wonderful woman, and always will hold a special place in my heart. For being a phenomenal mother, we're blessed to have you as family Matriarch. We are grateful to our pre-readers who participated in our book review process - your input elevated the book's value and purpose. Last, but certainly not least, I am grateful to our God, Creator, and Source for giving me life, grace, experience, and sanctification which lead me to my calling.

Introduction

Life is a journey of experiences, ups and downs, and adventures. As we get into our 50's and beyond, we have not only undoubtedly been through many life-altering transitions, from job loss, lack of career fulfillment, empty nest, divorce, loss of loved ones, financial shifts, to health concerns, but also the lack of relevance, passion, purpose, and socialization.

"Over 50, Starting Over" is both the journey of a man, Max Gilreath, and a joint collaboration. In his 50's, Max realized his life was not the dream he envisioned. After being laid off from a lucrative position in Corporate America, he sought out career counseling from transition and spiritual coach Deanna Poehlman. Her advice, guidance, and infectious passion helped him to look back at his life and recall, with introspection, his journey to date and find his true calling and passion.

"Over 50 Starting Over" use the analogy, "When we delay, postpone, or give up on our dreams and goals, we lose passion and purpose! It's like holding a beach ball under water; over time, the ball gets bigger and bigger until it has to surface!"

Vulnerable and candid, Max chronicles his life from his earliest recollections to present day. He unabashedly recounts the people, events and emotions that shaped him and the life transitions he's lived through. Conversely, Deanna's guidance, insight, and advice close each chapter, providing useful and practical ideas, suggestions, inspiration, and real-life examples.

Throughout the book, thought-provoking lists and questions allow the readers to evaluate, relate, and recount their own journey, becoming a cathartic experience on the road to identifying or reclaiming their own passion and purpose. Deanna's insights then help validate readers and fuel them to gain confidence and knowledge in navigating not only career transition but being authentic to their spiritual selves.

Now, at 60, Max has let go of the past, embraced the man he is today, and is living his passion and purpose. Deanna's guidance helped illuminate his path.

In this book, you will learn how to navigate through, and recover from, life's tough transitions while discovering ways to uncover your life's true purpose and how to go after it!

Having survived Corporate America, working for fortune 100 companies, Deanna left traditional work and a six-figure income in 2008 after coming to this realization: "I don't know what I'm going to do, but know what I am not going to do for even one more day". Shortly thereafter, she started her own consulting business and has helped hundreds find their lives' purpose, coaching them on how to transition into a career they love, and leading fulfilled lives.

After several years of Deanna's coaching through life's various transitions, Max reached out to her, asking her to co-author "Over 50, Starting Over". Their collective passion to help others through these transitions jumps off the pages in this book. The complete joy to witness first-hand the transformation from discouragement to gaining relevance, confidence, and happiness is what keeps this pair pining for more. Putting these passions into the written form allows Max and Deanna to reach the masses and aid many more people through the process.

Reading this book can also help you avoid these possible "Over 50" transitions by becoming aware of what may be up ahead and knowing how to create a proactive plan to live in your 50's, and beyond, on-purpose and joy-filled.

Life is a journey, full of transitions - you are not alone, and you have the power to re-image, re-imagine, and re-invent! So, turn the page, and allow your journey in "Starting Over" to begin.

Please feel free to share your stories and comments on our website:
www.over50startingover.net

CHAPTER ONE

A Bigger Life
Sink or Swim

"Over 50, Starting Over" can sound overwhelming! How do you start over, after 50 (or more) years of encountering peaks and valleys on life's roller coaster journey? Rejoice! You're not truly starting over; you're starting with a new perspective, a fresh approach, and a wealth of knowledge from all that you've already experienced.

Our 50's is often referred to as midlife. If we were to draw a line on a paper and put the number 50 in the middle, on the left side prior to 50, we'd have our developmental and childhood, teenager, and young adult years, along with vocational experience, relationships including marriage, children, and career. The prior to 50 half is typically filled with responsibilities, expectations, dependency (as in others depending on you) and pursuit. Life is often busy, hectic, and short on time.

Then, we hit midlife, and we reflect on the past. We may have an identity crisis; we've gotten so used to doing for others and ensuring their well-being, so we have to rediscover ourselves. What dreams and passions have we knowingly (or unknowingly) suppressed? How do we make the other side of 50 the life we dreamed of, the life that is destined for us? How do we work through the life-altering transitions and situations? Things like divorce, empty nest, job loss, societal and relational relevance, health concerns, loss of loved ones, financial shifts, and loss of socialization.

First, we need to know, at one time or another, we will all likely experience many of these situations and dealing with each of them is a life transition. The objective is to work through the transition, know that you are not alone and turn these transitions into transformations that uncover your true passion, your calling, and the path God has set out for you.

I have personally experienced all of these situations, and they are not easy. But, I have transitioned through them. I have transformed and am traveling on my passion journey. Before my true awakening, life was like trying to hold a beach ball under water - I use the following analogy as the underpinning of my story: *When we delay, postpone, or give up on our dreams and goals, we lose passion and purpose. It's like holding a beach ball under water; over time, the ball gets bigger and bigger until it has to surface!* Throughout the book, I have referred to the things that I delayed, postponed, or gave up on, as my "beach ball issues and challenges." In each decade of my life, I dealt with a new set of "beach ball issues and challenges".

The right side of the paper on which I put 50 in the middle is going to be no less significant than the left side, but it is now my life reimagined, re-imaged, and reinvented, vibrant with passion and purpose!

"Over 50, Starting Over" means you get to reset your expectations and perspectives for your dreams and passions. It's an opportunity to put everything you know through experience into action; it's an opportunity for change, learning, new beginnings, and growth as an expansion of yourself.

After more than 50 years of a life filled with many major transitions, I began to dig deeper into the true meaning of my being. I thought I knew me. After all, I was a highly successful professional, I had two boys who I adored and was so very proud of, and I garnered all of the material trappings of cliché societal success, but here I was in my late 50's, unemployed, feeling disappointed towards the overall corporate world that had taken so much of my life and made me dependent on it. The "corporate suits" trapped me with "golden handcuffs", shackled me to the currency train, and now they were not only releasing me, but they seemed to have forgotten me.

In the past, finding a job had not been such an arduous task. I had an enviable track record, and the calls and call backs were coming. But now, things were different; processing this change was becoming a bit overwhelming. I sought out help and guidance from a career, transition, and faith coach, and my dear friend, Deanna Poehlman. She asked me three questions that literally changed my life, "Max, what are you passionate about? What would make you jump out of bed every day enthused and excited? What do you want to do with your life?"

I pondered these questions, but yet I could not wholeheartedly reply. These three seemingly simple questions, at that juncture of my life, led me on a journey. A journey that took me back to childhood to reflect and understand the person I was, the person I had become, the challenges I dealt with, the transitions I lived through, the lessons I learned, and, most importantly and significantly, my true purpose and calling for the second half of my life.

Reconciliation was one of the first steps in the process of rediscovering who I am. I needed to reconcile the events and people in my life, and that meant I needed to forgive them *and* needed to forgive myself. I needed to divest myself from the heavy burden of anger and resentment. I needed to liberate myself in order to move forward. True forgiveness is so cathartic; while it does not mean you condone the wrong actions and/or bad behaviors, it allows you to wipe the slate clean and to create and paint the "Picasso" masterpiece of your life.

"Over 50, Starting Over" is like having every tool you will ever need to build anything you please - we just need to organize your toolbox and find out why you have accumulated what you have in experiences (good and bad) and how to gain additional resources to make every life transition you experience on purpose and joy-filled. The following life transitions and challenges had significant impact on my health and wellbeing. In my 50's, the cumulative effects had mounted to the point of crisis and a loss of real identity.

Divorce: More often than not, when we divorce in midlife, between the ages of 40 to 60, we may have been married for several years. In my case, it was twenty-two years. The longer we're married, the more settled we become to married life, one person, one relationship. If divorce happens at this time in our lives, we've been off the single "playing field" for a while. Society norms can shift and have probably evolved.

As in my situation, when I became single after 22 years of marriage, I was clueless to the dating landscape. When I dated my girlfriend who later became my wife, it was in the 70's, before the internet and digital age - it was practically "horse and buggy" era of dating compared to the 90s through the 2000s with all the social media and new internet paradigm. I had to start over, learning a new set of societal norms and interpersonal skills.

More than a half-century ago, only 2.8 percent of Americans older than 50 were divorced. By 2000, 11.8 percent were. According to the *2011 Census Bureau's American Community Survey,* 15.4 percent were divorced and another 2.1 percent were separated. Not to mention, some 13.5 percent were widowed.

Job Loss: If we lose our job later in life and find ourselves living on savings and investments, depleting our nest egg to survive over long periods of time, some of us are able to find a new job, but it usually is less and not equal to or greater than compensation we've grown accustomed to earning. Job loss for prolonged periods can result in taking any job in order to pay the bills. This can even mean taking positions in alternative industries, starting over with new learning curves and steep growth paths. Starting a new business, either out of want or necessity, can also be scary. Starting over to rebuild saving and nest egg in the aftermath of job loss can be frustrating. This is not where we thought we'd be at this time in our lives.

Relational Loss: The loss of a loved one, particularly a spouse or significant other can result in financial shifts, emotional and psychological challenges, and lack of socialization with others. We may start over learning how to live and cope without that person in our lives, trying to fill the void of their absence in a myriad of ways.

Empty Nest: The kids are gone, off to college or pursuing their own life's path. Just the two of you, starting over with a different and new relationship without the kids. What do you do with the time, energy, and space that was previously dedicated to the kids for years. Love for the kids does not change; however, love for each other may have been diminished, or, worse, simply lost.

- **Health Issues:** Health issues and challenges can arise at any time. For me, hypertension (high blood pressure), alcohol and tobacco addiction and abuse, prostate and kidney issues, liver complications, and depression had created Mind-Body-Spirit disconnects leading to poor health and wellness. I made the decision to start my life over, focused on a new perspective and approach to "total being" health. Depending on your health situation, starting over with new, or renewed, focus on health could be the difference between life and death.

- **Midlife Crisis:** The darkness of life can lead to unhealthy behaviors and crisis or loss of self. This can be an opportunity to start over with new behaviors and a healthier outlook. Does midlife crisis happen overnight or is it an evolved and building over time process? We will explore some of the causes and resolutions in subsequent chapters.

- **Loss of Relevance:** Loss of purpose, acceptance, and productivity can lead to isolation, dependency, and depression. Socialization and connection with others are critical for personal fulfillment. Starting over with "new glasses", or a fresh perspective, for maintaining existing relationships and creating new ones is essential to acceptance, caring, and sharing in life's second half.

- **Financial Shifts:** Job loss, health issues and the related cost, education cost, retirement, relational loss, midlife crisis, divorce, aging parents, and other life events can create financial shifts and challenges. At some point, many of us may experience the need to adjust and adapt to new economic shifts and different financial challenges. Starting over to adjust or rebuild the balance sheet may require a new approach, with a different standard of living.

Will our second half of life be better than the first half, or is the stage already set for new normative roles and expectations? The first half for many set anchor in disappointments and failed expectations. For others this period of life formed foundations for higher consciousness, self direction and personal growth. Both perspectives are determined by conscious and subconscious choices and decisions.

For me, who I was ten years ago is different from who (and what) I have become in my "Over 50" path and passage today. I had lived the first half dedicated to the external expectations of society, family, and community and giving up of my personal essence in a productive and constructive manner. Eager and impatient for a bigger life drove me to leave my small life behind, with commitment and expectations of myself, not from others. Over 50, my "passion inventory" was depleted, and I desperately needed a "life reset". Sink or swim? I chose to swim. Life transitions and imprints are the basis for this book, how experiences and lessons led me to find purpose and calling "Over 50".

These four building blocks are the keys for creating a new life with new passions "Over 50":

1. Decision to fully live, not merely exist or give up and die
2. Healthy Mind-Body-Spirit
3. Reconciliation/Forgiveness (of *both* self and others)
4. Legacy

Age and growing older are not death sentences. It's a matter of individual perspective, positive or negative. Aging should be viewed as the next (higher) level in life's evolution. After all, you're still alive. So, what stops people from embracing age with a positive outlook? "Starting Over" after 50 means you "get" to reset your expectations and perspectives for all of your future dreams and passions. It's an opportunity to put everything you now know through experience into action, and it's an important opportunity for change, learning, new beginnings, growth, and expansion of self.

Redefining our evolved life is not selfish or uncaring; rather, it's an introspective, realistic acceptance of our "now". Living your authentic self is the examination and explanation of your needs, wants, and desires. It starts with a singular decision to be honest with ourselves, then taking steps and actions for living our authentic selves. The rest will take care of itself, in a real and truthful way. The path to self truth can be riddled with doubt and fear; however, the outcomes can and will produce lasting peace and fulfillment.

We can carry the burden of living a life, based upon other's definitions and expectations, our own mistakes, failures, events, loss, and transitions. In midlife, my decision was "this is it"- fake it, stay the course and imagine living a successful life for everyone but myself. The outward me was successful, but the inward (authentic) me was out of balance and sorts.

We are consciously or subconsciously aware of what is wrong in our lives; however, so many of us don't understand why we refuse to change. Or worse, we deny there's anything amiss. Suppressing beach ball issues over years or decades, starts with early life's early experiences with ourselves and others. How we view others and how others view and influence us, creates our schema or framework. This framework develops our perceptions of the world and the people in it. How we adapt, adopt, contribute, and respond to life's events and transitions.

We may find ourselves "starting over" due to setbacks or reversal of progress, creating holding or "stuck patterns", impeding (or even paralyzing) natural life flow and fulfillment. I have experienced many of them, and every reader of this book has probably experienced at least one, maybe even many, of these transitions.

This book is much more than "how to" navigate life's midlife and older transitions; it's the story of what I've learned, and things you may consider, about navigating midlife turbulence while living and experiencing positive and sustainable outcomes. "Over 50" - midlife and senior years of life - are an opportunity for self actualization, resetting, retooling, and reconciliation. Throughout my adult life, I've sought out help and guidance both from professionals when I struggled to handle life's challenges on my own. Deanna has been one of those people. She has provided a guiding light through some of my darkest transitional hours, days, months, and years.

It's never too late to change perspective, take control, and live a bigger, more fulfilled, and meaningful life. Starting over is preserving what you've built, learned, and achieved over the years, while developing a blank canvas for creating and adding new capital, value, and perspective. My life's second half is greater and more fulfilling than the first. If I can do this, so can you. As we shed and reconcile the old, we can start fresh, making room for the new IF we understand that life's transitions and setbacks can become setups for life's true purpose and meaning. Here we go!

Reconciliation

The restoration of positive relationships is essential to the balance of healthy living. The action or process of forgiving (and/or being forgiven) is one of the most powerful and cathartic decisions we can make in life.

Forgiveness of others is more important to the forgiver than the person who is being forgiven. Why? Because it frees the forgiver of the burden, even if the person forgiven does not accept, or even knows of, the forgiveness. It is important to note that forgiveness does not mean you condone those wrong actions or behaviors.

Conversely, to be forgiven is the most profound act of grace and mercy. I have found in my own life to forgive and to be forgiven are both liberating, and yet the most liberating and profound form of forgiveness is in forgiving one's self. To release one's self from guilt, fault, and blame is a conscious decision to release internal feelings of self-condemnation.

We sometimes think self-punishment is the way to pay, or repent, for our transgression to others. This is a lie - self-punishment and regret only serve to create negative energies of guilt, sorrow, disappointment, and sadness. On the other hand, these same negative energies can manifest in blame towards others by transferring and projecting our pain.

The power of gratitude is *enormous*. To be thankful for life and all that we have is divine and spiritual. This positive energy attracts more positivity – good, positive people and things into our lives at the exact right moments, whereas negative thoughts and energy attracts those negative people and things.

Have you had the experience of engaging a negative person, and, upon departing their presence, felt drained of energy? I have learned to insulate my positive energy from this negativity by avoiding or deflecting those negative people or situations. And, Deanna also taught me the importance of separating people's actions from their behavior, or "third person" their behavior. Usually, there is a reason for their behavior that even they may not be aware of. This works by understanding we humans are all flawed, we all make mistakes, and not one of us is perfect. I've learned to practice this daily when engaging people. Deanna will further expand on this principle later.

There is a reason for people's behavior and a root cause or stimulus. The biggest challenge in my adult life was forgiveness - forgiving myself and forgiving a person who almost brought me to the point of hatred. I carried the emotional baggage of that situation for many years until I realized how much power that person and situation had over my life. I learned forgiveness for her through the actions of her son. If he could forgive her, then so could I.

The Inner Voice Is Getting Louder

    A few years ago, I needed an adventure, so I took a vacation to the Dominican Republic. It is a small island country located in the Caribbean, a beautiful tropical country of Spanish and African culture with a population of approximately four million.

    Needing space and separation from my usual daily routine, I decided to visit a country where I could visualize and immerse my dream of living abroad. The Dominican Republic (DR) is a beautiful country known for its majestic beaches, roaming countryside, vibrant rainforest, fine cigars, and abundant agriculture. In my travels, I discovered a small island town named Boca Chica – it has white sand beaches and sparkling blue-green water, with people who are very kind-hearted and hospitable.

    My mind and spirit felt open and free in Boca Chica, and I made reservations at a local resort to spend time there to reinvigorate, reflect, and regenerate. Shortly after arriving at the resort, I was greeted by a tall, lanky man, possibly in his 70s, with a big smile, and, "Hi! How are you today?" His energy was so positive, real, and sincere. Turns out, he was the maintenance man for the resort.

    The DR, like many Latin American countries, is a blend of first- and third-world infrastructure and economy. With a median income of approximately $400 USD per month, the DR is mostly rich and poor with very little middle class.

    Here was this man with very little financial means, and yet he's genuinely happy, with an infectious smile and personality. I seldom see rich or wealthy people in America with that kind of joy and happy spirit. His energy stayed with me all day, and we greeted each other with the same positive energy and joy every day of my stay. He inspired me and still does.

    The DR has some of the most beautiful sunrises and sunsets in the world. On my last day of my visit to Boca Chica, I awoke early to experience the 6:00AM sunrise. It was dawn with a light breeze as I walked to the beach, and no one else was at the beach except a property security guard. I could hear the slight sound of fish jumping in and out of the water as if joyfully greeting the new day. It was a surreal moment - everything was in slow motion, and all of my senses were heightened and alive. I said my prayer and gave thanks for my life.

Then, on cue, the sun began to slowly rise with blended streams of brilliant colors of crimson, orange, blue, purple, yellow, and pink, all blending and moving, then disappearing into the bright sunlight. What was most captivating to me was how quickly it all took place - only six minutes for the transformation. I call it "God showing out!"

The change of color and the transformation of dark to light touched my soul, because, in those moments, I thought about all the dark times in my life and how they always transformed to beauty and light. In those moments, I realized how much I changed over the years and how blessed I truly am. Yes, I'm thankful to be alive.

I visited different resorts in another beach town named Juan Dolio, where I had an additional inspiring experience. While walking the beach where panhandling is a frequent occurrence, I noticed a man waving at me with a big smile. He appeared to be between thirty to thirty-five years old. Upon closer view, I could see, though he had no legs from the torso down, he managed his mobility by using his arms and hands as his legs and feet.

As I approached him, his smile became more luminous. After our introduction, he shared with me he could not be out in the sun for very long because of the heat, which was approximately ninety degrees. We chatted for a few minutes, and while he did not ask me for money, I told him I didn't have any money with me. However, I added if he would be at the beach the next day, I would bring him some money. I looked for the man when I made it back to the beach, but I never saw him again during the remainder of my stay.

The experience had a profound effect on me, one of inspiration, empathy, and gratitude. This is a man with half of a body, accepting his plight is a part of his daily life (I'm not sure I would say suffering because of his true joy). So many of us have so much, and yet we complain about every little thing, and enough is never enough. This man's heart was FULL!

I ask you who has the more fulfilled and meaningful life? The man with half a body who gets joy from simply having a conversation with strangers and joyfully greeting others with a FULL HEART, or the person who has financial resources, good health, family and friends, but no gratitude for their blessings, and does nothing to give back or help others?

These two people inspired me to be more thankful for everything, and I still continue to do so. Gratitude for life and what it gives us every day tells the universe we are thankful for all that it gives. No matter our situation or circumstance, we always have something or someone to be thankful for. I say, "Thank you!" *out loud* many times a day. I once read Albert Einstein would say, "Thank you." many times daily, in gratitude for his unique brain abilities. Gratitude overcomes and often brings overwhelming blessings!

Gratitude does not covet others but allows them to make their own paths and define their happiness. The two inspirational gentlemen I encountered appeared to have done just that: They defined their happiness, and they share it with others. I would not describe their situation as misfortune; rather, I would define it as they are grateful for what they do have and have accomplished.

The maintenance man appears happy in spirit, as he has a job and gets to meet new people and spread cheer. The man without legs is likely content he has developed a strong upper torso so he has mobility, and he likely enjoys talking to people and being able to witness and experience the natural beauty of the beach, the water, the sky, the town, and the myriad of visitors. I observed a common thread from both men: Their genuine smile and positive peaceful energies, generated despite their life's circumstances. I sensed an inner peace and gratitude for life itself.

True growth in the soul is when we can reflect on our negative experiences, viewing them as challenges we overcame and reminding us to be grateful for the positive experiences.

Stubbornness, self-pity, anger, lack of our own accountability - these are roadblocks that stop us from acknowledging and enjoying so many of life's blessings. Through my divorce, I unintentionally hurt the people I love most, and bore its burden deep within my heart. After 50, I began to take inventory of my most important life's relationships, and seek answers and resolution to my inner torments, like:

A. While there were many things I wish would have been different in my relationship with my parents, life's journey has given me a greater respect and understanding of them and the situations they faced. My reflection now is sadness they did not appear to give me more of themselves through their love and nurturing. In my maturity and clarity, I began to understand and recognize the gifts from my parents in my life. Though unintentionally given, their teachings have helped guide my life's path. I had to live and experience life in order to understand and apply that wisdom.

B. Divorce was the biggest internal torment of my life and had the most negative impact over anything I've experienced. Why? Because I blamed myself for the divorce and the impact it had on my sons, and because I love them beyond measure. However, it also had lessons and revelations for me:

- The power of our creator
- The power of love
- Asked for forgiveness
- Received forgiveness
- Forgave myself

What I Learned:
- The enemy is ourselves
- Power of forgiveness and reconciliation, moving on, going forward with love
- Gratitude, giving thanks for all things - good *and* bad - for they make me who I am today

Legacy

Every living thing is in a constant state of change; otherwise, it dies. And, in actuality, death is just another state of change. People's perspective on their personal aging process is healthy, unhealthy, or indifferent. Healthy focus is on the total person: Mind-Body-Spirit. Unhealthy is a singular focus on the Mind-Body-Spirit. People naturally tend to shift their focus from the physical to the mental and spiritual as they age.

I did not have a real focus on my legacy until my 50s. Why? Because I finally faced the reality of mortality. One day, I will die (and, so will you). So, how do I want to be remembered by the people who matter most to me? What did I do that left a lasting, positive imprint on their lives? Will I leave this life with healthy and positive personal relationships?

Putting others before yourself is the most selfless thing you can do in life. This is now my focus...and freedom. My father would say, ***"The best sermon that I ever experienced was the one that I saw and not heard."*** I want people to remember what I did through my actions that positively impacted their lives.

One of my passions is to create a homestead property in Costa Rica for my sons and their spouses, my grandchildren, allowing my family and friends to enjoy nature-based living for generations to come. The dream of living abroad with dual citizenship (US and Costa Rica) facilitates my need for simplicity and love of nature.

Costa Rica is considered to be one of the world's most beautiful countries. With large Centenarian populations. There are areas where poor people seem to be aging more slowly, than wealthier people elsewhere. People can live 2 to 3 years longer, than other Costa Ricans. One primary reason for extended longevity is, family and social connections, which make older people feel needed. Family and social support are important are important no matter where we live.

Advantages of living abroad:
- Extended life expectancy
- Personal growth
- Experience multi-cultural lifestyles
- Meet cohort communities

What I Learned:
- Listen to and trust my inner voice
- Legacy - what will live on after I'm gone
- Leave nothing undone (or unsaid)

Calling

"Calling: When what you really want to do is the same as who you really are."
- Max Gilreath

To me, a calling is a strong, inner inclination toward a particular course of action, especially when accompanied by conviction and/or divine influence. Life is not a destination; it is a journey composed of failures, successes, and lessons, with a season for every phase of life.

Life's evolution into my 50's has presented an amazing opportunity for introspection and understanding of who I really am. I value my life now more than I ever have, in part because there's so much I (still) want to do.

My core qualities - insightful, spiritual, creative, love and visionary - are the same as my passion and advocacy for older and aging people. When who you really are is the same as that you do, defines calling. It always come from the heart. When you clearly identify your life's calling and take action, it can be one of the most fulfilling and rewarding contributions to yourself and others you can make.

The deeper one's self-love, the more one is aware of one's personal calling and what it takes to act on that calling. Every person who I've known or observed who acted on their calling had one thing in common: PASSION!

What I Learned:
- We are all special, and we each have a unique calling
- I received my purpose and calling in the second half of my life, when I had the wisdom and experience to act on it
- What faith really means to me

Redefining Success

I have never heard any two people give the same definition for success, because it means something different to everyone. To me, success is an evolving description - one that, at least in my own life, has been driven by external stimuli. For example, when I entered Corporate America in my twenties and thirties, the trappings of success were based upon income, title, home, neighborhood, cars, clothes, affluence, and upward mobility.

In my forties, after divorce, and the process of empty-nesting, my definition slowly began to change towards intrinsic evaluation of self and life's meaning. Less is more, and the simpler, the better. I know people who now are in their 50's and 60's, with empty nest, who still live in large homes with multiple bedrooms and furnishings which seldom are used or appreciated. Why? Maybe because their "things" could possibly represent personal status and success to them.

Most likely, it's important to them how others perceive them, and there is the need to keep up appearances. Perhaps it is derived from tradition, their parents stayed in the same house they raised their family in until their deaths. It also could be they fear the acknowledgment they are in a new chapter of their life; one that is not responsible for others' wellbeing. It may be a residual effect of coming to terms with the empty nest, or it may be the house that holds so many past treasured memories it is symbolic for them and downsizing truly signals moving on and accepting their children are now adults. (I have several friends in N.Y. who took 5-7 years before they moved from their very large homes into a home that was more manageable and suitable. Some of the reasons they cited are the memories the home held for them, a way to hold onto the younger version of their now-adult children.)

As the saying goes, "to each, their own", and I'm at peace with my choices, content as a single man in my one bedroom apartment where I only have what I need and every inch of space is utilized. It is truly what works for me. Analyze your situation and find what works best for you.

How I define success now, at almost 60?

- Simplicity
- Freedom
- Authenticity - inner peace
- Healthy Mind-Body-Spirit
- Happy and healthy family
- Self-love, comfortable in my skin
- Passion for life, dreams, purpose, and meaning

If you're "Over 50" this is an opportunity to finally get your life right. Or to learn how to transition from one good part to the next great part? Life without passion for who you are and what you want to do is a self-imposed form of death. Through the years, I learned Corporate America was not the dream I envisioned, but it was part of the journey that got me here, to today – wiser, focused, and appreciative of my life with passion.

In my 50's, I decided I could no longer afford *not* to change, so I embraced my own individual life's path and calling. I did it! And, so can you! Release the passion within you. Your calling and idea of success are as unique as your fingerprint. Aging process may create a paradox of internal conflict. Blessed and unfulfilled at the same time, navigating life with an internal compass "stuck" in an east/west, lateral position, and in need of repair and reset for a more northerly direction.

I believe we have two prime of life periods: 1.) Youth-based, when we are at the peak of our powers and physical abilities. 2.) Experience-based, when wisdom, accomplishment, and our Mind-Body-Spirit health are in transition to transformation or decline. Like any good story, we all have a beginning, middle, and end. There are definite reasons why life's journey in the second half is either fulfilling or not. We can run but we can't hide, at least not from ourselves. I chose to change and move on, into my calling and destiny. ***My biggest obstacle has been me.***

Things to Consider:

Know your value. We should all know our non-negotiable principles. Know your passions, wants, needs and calling for your life. Write them down below, in your personal log, diary, memoir, or electronic file, etc. Fresh, new passion, and positive energy can redefine success in the second half.

Notes and Affirmations:

_____
_____
_____
_____
_____
_____
_____
_____
_____
_____

Deanna's Coaching and Encouragement

Forgiveness and reconciliation - those are heavy topics that come with even heavier action plans. Forgiveness is what I call and encourage as "non-negotiable". It will/can end up manifesting into the largest percentage of air space in your beach ball. As Max mentioned, forgiveness has nothing to do with the person you are forgiving and everything to do with you.

If you have been to a Protestant Church more than ten times in your life, you most likely heard a more stinging version of this forgiveness exercise, which is: "How can you expect God to forgive you of your sins if you are not willing to forgive those who sin against you?". It is simply non-negotiable and requires change of heart geared toward moving forward and "Starting Over".

Some people do not like to hear, nor do they acknowledge, some things simply are not an option. Of course, you have an option; although, the option of not forgiving comes with the displeasure of what I call "blocking blessings", it's still *your* "option". I do not mean to imply that if you are obedient, then the blessings automatically flow. We serve a Creator and God who is not transactional. If God were small enough to understand, He wouldn't be grand enough to worship. But, to be disobedient is a whole other thing.

Something that has made it easier for me to forgive others comes from one of my many favorite quotes from Dr. Phil (and Eleanor Roosevelt): "You wouldn't worry what people thought of you if you knew how seldom they did!". When we hurt from being wronged by others, we often think they are thinking of us, perhaps of more ways to hurt us, or just celebrating in what they did or said. But, what really goes through our mind eventually is: "Why haven't they apologized? Why don't they understand how hurtful they were?" And, so on… Our enemy wants us to continually "park" our mindset on all of that hurt and all of the pain. It is non-negotiable to continue to *volunteer* to be our own enemy anymore! Besides, we wouldn't worry about what people thought of us if we knew how seldom they actually did (worth repeating!).

Forgiveness is such a wonderful gift from God. His forgiveness and reconciliation is the ultimate love and most perfect gift. Remember, our journey here is a head-start to our future and continued journey in Heaven.

God wants us to learn the act of forgiveness, so that we may attempt to understand and comprehend the depths of where His forgiveness comes. Our hurt pales in comparison to the broken heart of Jesus when we refuse to forgive and continue to succumb to emulating our enemy's heart and not our Lord's!

Now, on reconciliation, there are some relationships that we are not recommended to reconcile with. Forgiveness does **NOT** mean you are signing up for additional pain, abuse and bullying! It does not mean you condone the bad behavior. Understand this: *Some of the people we forgive in life will not come with a full reconciliation.* We teach people how to treat us. Some relationships will be left in our past (with full forgiveness) and will be chalked up to lessons learned and wisdom gained. It may be our generation, but I have found that people thought when you truly forgive someone who has wronged you that you *must* jump back in there with the relationship and begin where you left off. That is just simply not the case. When you extend and sincerely acknowledge forgiveness, you do not have to sign up to endure more hurt, shame, etc.

How liberating and freeing is the truth of forgiveness? Forgive, communicate the new boundaries (if necessary), and pray for them. When you do forgive, most of the air in the burdened, heavy, exhausting beach ball will be gone!

Max mentioned my reference to "third-person" in coaching. I'd like to expand on that concept for you. Every day, every minute, every second actually, we are making real-time choices (either consciously or subconsciously) to follow our enemy, or our God. With every thought, action, word, expression, etc. We either sign-up to work for God, or sign-up to work for Satan. That reminds me of a saying I once heard and still love: Be the kind of person who when you wake up every day and your feet hit the floor, the devil says, "Oh crap, s/he's up!".

But, our enemy knows us well. He will roam our friends, colleagues, family, neighbors, and strangers, to look for a willing volunteer to attempt to kill, steal, and destroy us! Unfortunately, there are many who sign-up. However, when dealing with people and relationships, especially those we love, I like to envision THEY are not the enemy, because they simply are not.

They just temporarily (or, in some cases, permanently), sign-up to work for and with our enemy who is against us. So, it is much easier to think of them as just the vessel that temporarily worked for our enemy because every hurt, all bad things that are done to us come directly from our enemy, not God's beloved sons and daughters (and remember, we are all His beloved). So, next time you are being wronged, or someone is being hateful to you, remember to "third-party" or "third-person" it - truly, it is not them, but our enemy working through them/us.

Gratitude. Talk about a "grace tank" filler! Gratefulness (and thankfulness) is a most vital mindset for the process of "Starting Over". Actually, for life itself, a grateful heart is essential. Being thankful and having joy have nothing to do with our circumstances. In fact, the Bible tells us in James (and I'm paraphrasing here) that even when trouble of any kind come our way, we need to consider it as an opportunity for great joy. You will find a spirit of gratitude is the cornerstone and an important element in both being happy and living a joy-filled, purpose-driven, and abundantly blessed life.

"Let gratitude be the pillow upon which you kneel to say your nightly prayer. And let faith be the bridge you build to overcome evil and welcome good."
- Maya Angelou

Now that we have forgiven, are reconciled, and thinking with a grateful, thankful heart, it is time to assess our personal successes. I'm not sure why some of us "Over 50" default our thinking as to our lack of ability to be a valued contributor. After all, after 50, we have 50 years of success that I'm certain carves out a pattern of accomplishment.

How we define personal success can vary, not necessarily the typical societal adages, but, for instance, raising our children, helping to put a customer presentation in order, keeping our home organized, managing a successful team, volunteering, or helping neighbors - whatever it is we can be proud of and excited about putting our name on, especially those accomplishments that will make Jesus proud of us. Assessing these achievements can segue to discovering your calling and help determine what it is you are to do as a vocation. When you chart out these personal successes, I'm willing to guess you will find a pattern and legacy of positive contribution which will result in a renewed sense of personal value and purpose.

Here is where your beach ball meets the sand. It is decision time. Are you going to sink or swim? Are you going to be a victim or victor? Are you going to claim the blessings laid out for you that are just in your reach if you stretch yourself, custom-made for your heart? Or, are you going to keep believing the enemy's lies?

My prayer for you: May you run fast and hard after what you know it is you were born to do, praying **with abundant faith** - Matthew 21:22. (I'll let you look that up.) ☺

CHAPTER TWO

"Something Special"
Markers That Color My Life

Despite the dreaded anticipation of the needle, the young boy intently listened to the doctor and his mother's conversation. Even to the ears of a child terrified by what's to come, he has a sense of calm purely engendered by the friendly and familiar rapport between the doctor and his mother. Today, as nearing being a 60-year-old man, he remembers this process taking approximately 15 minutes. However, the words spoken by the physician would last a lifetime - he said, "Ms. Gilreath, out of all of your children, this boy has something special to offer the world!"

After the prick of the needle and its sting were over, the doctor wiped the spot of blood with an antiseptic, applied a Band-Aid, patted the boy on the back, and said, "Take care, young man." The boy's mother had a pleasant smile with a look of anticipating the next task for the day on her face. Born to this world and its reality called LIFE, a conscious awareness of his senses and himself washed over him.

Processing the doctor's words about this young boy and his future was profound. Did the boy have something special to offer the world? Was the doctor foretelling his future? Little did the boy know he would not learn the answer to this question until he reached his 50's, proving it's never too late to find answers to life's most important questions. The boy's memory is vivid: Starting at age 5, this prediction would resonate with the young boy, from his youth into adulthood, serving as a guiding principle and *marker* throughout his life.

That young boy was me, and this is my story of my life's journey and how it may be of benefit in your life, no matter your age. Looking back, I was a "momma's boy". I sought the security and comfort of my mother's touch and her sweet, familiar voice. I enjoyed watching and learning from her. I needed my mother's attention - I wanted her to see me as "special." When the doctor said I'm special - that was my first "aha" moment. When he said I was special - I wanted to be special to my mother. And, when he said I had something special to offer the world, that was a big deal to me then (and has been all of my life). More than half century later, the impact of that moment is distinctly vivid in both my mind and heart.

In those few moments with my mother at the doctor's office, I experienced my first understanding of self-actualization. In the tender mind of a young boy, I pondered the questions: WHY am I here? What is life? Even as a boy, I began the pursuit of self-awareness, esteem, fulfillment, and building blocks to middle age.

Have you pondered the meaning of your life and WHY you're here? Many people, at some point in their life, have asked themselves these questions. It's natural to be curious and inquisitive about existence itself.

In youth, we are inquiring and imaginative about the wonders of life. Then, when we grow up, life can overwhelm our sense of what happiness (and being happy) is and really means. In childhood innocence we ponder the mysteries of life, in the moment and in real-time. Recognizing and understanding why and how we've developed over the years, can become the building blocks for introspective change.

It took more than half a century to understand what "something special" really means for me, and knowing in my heart that the pains and hurts of life can result in calling for a higher purpose. And, part of my higher purpose is revealing my life's experiences and learning in the service of mankind

We all have "something special" in our being, that yearns to be set free, used and lived out. It is our desire you make space for calling and awakening in your life.

What I Learned:
- Identifying the core events and experiences in life that make you who you are today
- Most people have issues and problems, no matter how perfect his/her life may appear on the outside. We're all struggling with something
- Life is meant to be filled with happiness and joy throughout, not just in youth or at specific times and events
- Why am I here? What do I want to achieve and then leave as a legacy? What is my life's calling?

It's never too late - *"Give up, give in, or give it all you've got."*
- Anonymous

For me, each decade (thus far) had an imprint, new experiences, personal growth, and development. My experiences in the 1960's and 1970's were most influential in establishing the foundation for the man I would become.

As human beings, we absorb positive (and repel negative) situations, events, and experiences in our lives. Painful experiences and memories can be the most difficult to reconcile. It's how we *choose* to process, articulate, and translate their long-term meanings that set the stage for individual development and growth...or stagnation and loss of hope.

The World is Bright and Full of Promise

The '60's was a decade of huge social and political change in America:

Civil Rights and Conflict:
    First Man on the Moon
    Anti-War Movement
    Hippies
Political Assassinations:
    John F. Kennedy
    Robert Kennedy
    Martin Luther King, Jr.

America had entered a time of upheaval, turmoil, and change, an ethos driven by war and the fight for human rights and freedom. However, life in the American South, in the sixties, was also simple, faith-based, honest, and hard-working. The American workers and employers were loyal to each other, and the norm was to have two, or maybe three, jobs in your entire adult life.

My parents were "salt of the earth" people – typical of the South. My father was an auto mechanic, who owned an auto repair and body shop on our property for more than 50 years. He and his brother took great pride in their work – they worked long hours, were respected in the community, and never met a stranger. Dad was an Army World War II Veteran, strong-willed and independent. Dad was a businessman and entrepreneur who refused to ever work for anyone other than himself.

On the other hand, my mother, having given birth to nine children, was a housewife, until her 50's. Then, she became a housekeeper, working outside the home. She also earned her driver's license for the time ever. Shortly thereafter, when my younger brother and I were older and more self-sufficient, she worked at one of the local factories to earn more money to support the family. My mother was a quiet and humble woman, yet she had the spunk and savvy of a warrior.

In retrospect, she was "Over 50, Starting Over", entering the workforce, and learning to drive. To my knowledge, the combined incomes from both my parents never exceeded $20k annually; however, they owned land, had a mortgage-free home, and little to no installment loan or debt of any kind.

While $20K in the 60's and 70's is better than decent income, having a large family would still require them to be very prudent with their finances. Owning land without a mortgage based on this income with a family of this size is a great accomplishment. In addition, neither of my parents completed their high school education. Yet, they were extremely smart and sensible.

As the eighth of nine siblings, I learned so much from observing my older brothers and sisters - they were my family role models. If we were all alive, our ages would range from 58 to 79; thus, we're middle age, barely "boomer", and mostly senior. Being next to last in the sibling line-up, I learned early on to be self-reliant and independent. While I was very close to the siblings who were nearest to me in age, they all had traits and characteristics I admired, especially my older brother "Chip".

My spiritual and religious foundation came from my parents. I grew up Methodist but developed into a non-denominational church member in my 20's. I believe in God; however, I'm spiritual more than "religious" and tend to have "live and let live" as a primary philosophy.

One of my fondest memories growing up was going to Sunday School, followed by the regular church service, and then a trip into town with my younger brother and parents for ice cream cones. My father would always stop to buy the latest "Muscle and Fitness" magazine. Physical fitness was very important to him. I later realized this was a form of escape, even therapy, for his life. Many people find a way to escape, or numb, the pains of life in a myriad of ways. Large families in those days may have had relative sibling and parent separations, due to age, roles and responsibilities and order within the birth cycle.

Here are a few things social psychologists have mentioned regarding large families of the twenty first century: In large families, those more attuned to and acutely aware of the lack of parental involvement often seek acknowledgement of self-worth in other areas. I got my self-worth from athleticism and oratory public speaking skills. Any form of a better socio-economic life is routinely discouraged in large families. The culture of large families usually emphasizes just the basic human needs of food, clothing, and shelter.

My sisters were great with assisting our mother with routine family tasks. College and the importance of education were not discussed in our family. My siblings and I wanted more in life than "just the basics"; we wanted more - to have some of the things we saw others enjoy. And, the only way to achieve all of those things was to leave our hometown. I think, subconsciously, we wanted to escape the reminders of the socio-economic status we grew up in. Ultimately, at one time or another, we all escaped...or made peace with it.

Some social psychologists in the twentieth century have stated, "Parents of large to very large families are indeed (often) uninvolved, unavailable, and non-nurturing." Looking back, I realized I had low self-esteem primarily based upon my family's financial position, which seemed low income (despite the size of our family), in comparison to other middle and upper-middle class families in my small hometown of less than 20,000 - Wilkesboro, North Carolina (There's also a North Wilkesboro - they are distinctively different).

Throughout my school-age years, I felt I did not fit in; my classmates came from families who appeared to have much greater financial resources than my family. It made me feel uncomfortable and not on their economic or social level. This made me feel isolated, even ashamed. At the time, it felt as if others thought I was beneath them. I did not fit into the socio-economic, status-based groups and cliques of my peers throughout my formal education experience.

There were six trajectories and events between ages 10 and 21 which molded my evolution from boyhood to becoming a man.

You too may have a list of molding events. So, consider making a list and see the possible correlation with your life's transitions and challenges.

1. I am Athletic
   - Gave me confidence and provided potential athletic scholarship funding for college
2. I am a Public Speaker
   - Gave me dignity and confidence builder
3. I am High School Class Vice President
   - Gave me relevance - I was as good as the other students, and I could be a leader
4. I am Going to College
   - College was the ticket out of my hometown into a new life
5. I am a Father
   - I have responsibility for someone other than myself - my kids would have a better life than I had, and they will know that I love them equally
6. I am a Husband
   - I'm in love and caring for the mother of my children

Throughout my life, there have been many experiences per decade that have molded and changed me for the better:

70's
High School and College
- Low self-esteem: Am I worthy of success and good things?
- Discovery of talents
- Preparing to leave my hometown for college and new life
- Marriage and fatherhood
- Huge responsibility

- Accelerated growth to manhood
- Leaving home – Travel
- Exploration
- Provide for my family
- Career and life opportunities
- Independence
- New experiences
- Possibilities

The 80's
Family and Career
- Family
- Career
- Money
- Opportunity
- Personal growth
- Focus on health and Mind-Body-Spirit

The 90's
Death, Divorce, and Career and Financial Transitions
- Divorce was devastating, and it was challenging to keep moving forward
- Dealing with the loss and grief over my parents' deaths and gaining a greater understanding and appreciation to be the best parent I can be
- Emotional tumult, reaching deep into my core to deal with two of the most difficult transitions in life - death and divorce
- Need for Growth
- Go from Houston, Texas to Los Angeles, California for greater career, family, and social growth and development
- Entrepreneurial ventures
- Explore my passions and new perspectives
- Fulfillment

The 2000's
I'm getting older and sense a shift in the purpose and meaning for my life

- Loss of employment or job transition
- Financial setback
- Loss of loved ones - death of two of my brothers
- The Path to 50 and midlife - what those meant to me
- Mortality - acknowledging our time is finite and ruminating on my legacy

The 2010's
Major Transition
- Financial Transition
- Confidence Reborn: Working through the emotions and setbacks of the previous decade and emerging stronger and more confident.
- Rebirth and calling
- Contentment in simplicity and becoming less materialistic

We derive much of ethics, moral compass and behaviors based on our environment in our developmental years, which is most influenced by our parents. Here's what I've rejected and learned from mine:

What I Rejected From My Parents

Negative things from my Mother:
- My perception was she did not give as much love to me as my siblings
- Lack of parental guidance for my education and basic life teachings
- Fear - her generation allowed the negative images of television to rob them of many life's adventures and pleasures such as commercial flight. However, she was fearless when it came to her own "comfort zone", or the world that she controlled

Negative things from my Father:
- Anger
- Regret - he internalized his lack of opportunity to achieve more
- Fear of the unknown outside his localized "comfort zone"
- Lack of knowledge to display love and affection
- Lack of knowledge to communicate

- o Did not finish what he started - he had vision and ability without the financial means to complete
- o Lack of parental attention based upon the size of our family and limited financial resources
- o Negative outlook
- o Negative relationship to money - he always spoke of the sin and greed of money, and allowed patrons to cheat him out of their debt to him, because he extended credit. (This was before credit cards, and he trusted to a fault.) People took his kindness for weakness
- o Did not like change
- o Lacked vision for planning for the well-being of his children (but this goes back to how he was raised)

What I Learned From My Parents

Good things from my Mother:
- o She loved my father
- o Kind to others
- o Untiring work ethic
- o Determination
- o Doer
- o Patience
- o Intellect
- o Faith
- o How to plan
- o Positive outlook
- o Tenacity
- o Healthy living
- o Discipline
- o How to create visual appeal - she always put her best foot forward

Good things from my Father:
- o He loved my mother
- o Physical and nutritional health
- o Pragmatic wisdom
- o Perseverance

- o Resilience
- o Untiring work ethic
- o Kind heart
- o Curiosity for mechanical and engineering disciplines
- o Analytical
- o Faith

These experiences and teachings helped arm and prepare me for the transitions to come. Yet I would need the help of others to persevere and survive.

My oldest brother served as my first role model. His nickname was "Chip", and I wanted to emulate him. Approximately 10 years older than I am, Chip was the first to leave our hometown - this showed me I could do it too. He entered the Navy in the early 1960's as the first sibling to officially leave our small hometown and not return to live after his career ended.

As a black teenager, he became my hero as an example of success, and I could totally relate to this version of achievement because he was my brother, because he had the courage to leave the family, to leave the city, even to leave the country, and because I envisioned him having great experiences and seeing the world.

I was (and still am) extremely proud of him. Chip traveled around the world during his 20-plus-year career. Our family received postcards and letters from Spain, Australia, and the Philippines to name only a few countries. I had only read about them in school or seen them on TV or in the movies. He was like our family's "James Bond": Handsome, worldly, and smart. His experience was the catalyst that fueled my passion to find a way to escape what felt like a dead-end that awaited me after high school. I wanted go to college, find a career, and travel.

So, in 1969, at age 13, I set the following goals for my high school years:

1. Get a summer job to buy my first car at age 16
2. Become high school student body president
3. Become a top track & field athlete and get a college athletic scholarship
4. Leave North Carolina

In 1970, something very exciting happened for my older sister and me. We were invited to go with our aunt and uncle to visit extended family in Ontario, Canada. WOW, I was beside myself! I'm actually going to visit a foreign country - just like my older brother, Chip. I could not wait for the opportunity!

We drove from North Carolina to Detroit Michigan, over the Ambassador Bridge, and into Ontario Canada; the whole trip over 16 hours. We arrived at our cousin's home in the land of maple leaves and hockey approximately 5:00am and knocked on the door. When that door opened, a middle-aged, white woman greeted us with open arms.

I'm in Canada and I have white relatives! Double WOW! No one had told us of our multiracial family tree. After getting over my initial surprise, I learned my Canadian relatives were on my mother's side, where interracial marriages had occurred. The trip to Canada inspired me and further fueled my desire to learn more about this big world.

Visiting Canada at such a young age was my first experience with socialization beyond the state of North Carolina and America, and experiencing a foreign society. This gave me confidence to travel, communicating and engaging different people and new things.

In turn, I gained a higher awareness in the world, realizing for the first time there was always a bigger life beyond the norm. It provided new perspective for viewing future challenges and transitions from different angles and points of view. What was most surprising to me was the utter absence of racism or bigotry. It opened my mind to empathy for others and helped to create a desire for setting goals and achievement. Thus, achieving my high school goals became even more urgent and important.

Here, I had experienced a foreign country, just like my brother "Chip" a young "007". To this very day, I never knew who orchestrated and initiated the trip - my aunt and uncle or my parents. And, why my sister and I were selected out of all my family? I've simply accepted the fact that it was supposed to happen.

Many people have unexplained life-changing experiences. What are yours?

_____

_____

_____

Caught In the Quicksand of Anger

Certain traits we consistently see in our core family have profound effects on us. Every family has both positive *and* negative traits. As a young man, however, I thought it was just my family who had more negative traits than positive ones. So often, it seemed my father was either angry or had an "aura of anger", and it left an imprint on me such that it became one of my biggest challenges to date. To better understand this anger, to deal with it, and to not let it consume me, I had to find a way to manage it.

Anger, as defined by the American Psychological Association (APA), is an emotion characterized by antagonism toward someone or something you feel has deliberately done you wrong. Anger *can* be a good thing in that it can give you a way to express negative feelings or motivate you to find solutions to problems. But, excessive anger or uncontrolled rage can cause more problems than they solve.

Increased blood pressure and other physical changes associated with anger make it difficult to think straight and harm your physical health and mental well-being. My father lacked self-esteem primarily because of his life's circumstances, prejudice, lack of education and opportunity, which transferred to me. This cycle of oppression and suppression, started long before him, they were generational, with little progress to break the cycle. Anger!

Yes, people can transfer their issues and behaviors to others, both knowingly and unknowingly, intentionally and unintentionally. As a child, and later as a teen, I learned, and even absorbed, anger and low self-esteem. As I matured into adulthood, I acknowledged my self-esteem needed an overhaul and was determined not to get mired down in the quicksand of that same anger and low self-esteem anymore.

I decided to "Start Over", reinvent, and recreate myself, becoming the person I believed I was destined to be. One thing is for sure - I was not going to sing the sad song I commonly heard from older people: "Coulda, Woulda and Shoulda!"

I "coulda" been so much more in life!

**I "woulda" never given that company my best years!
I "shoulda" left him or her years ago!**

I refer to these people as "CWS" people! Their life's journeys are filled with blaming others, living in the past, and, in some cases, living a lie; they are miserable and want to make everyone and everything miserable along with them. After all, "misery loves company."

I learned early in life I could choose between a miserable life versus one filled with passion, meaning, and adventure. I chose passion, meaning, and adventure. But, "life's journey", if you like, has a way of picking the "passion pocket", slowly eroding one's optimism and zeal. However, I decided becoming a "CWS" person was not, and still is not, an option!

Over the years, when faced with situations beyond my understanding or control, I've engaged the services of professionals specializing in that area of need. When we're sick, we go to the doctor; need legal assistance, we get an attorney, etc. One such professional resource I've needed from time to time has been that of a "Life Coach", someone to provide strategies and techniques to achieve my life's goals and objectives.

Deanna has been that resource for me, as an investment in my life's journey. Her valuable career coaching and forthright advice have been particularly effective in navigating today's new digital job market and helping me to understand my value, my worth, and my self-branding. Deanna was instrumental in forming my "unique value proposition" which we'll discuss later on in more detail.

She very effectively uses the analogy of holding a beach ball under water: When we divert, postpone, or give up on our dreams and goals, we lose passion and purpose. That is like holding a beach ball under water. Over time, that ball gets bigger and bigger until it has to surface. Deanna provides effective, useful tools and workable examples for creating a new life that is passionate and full of purpose - no matter what challenges or situations you're faced with, you can change. On-purpose living helps you define, create, and release your passion.

My beach ball challenges at ages 18 to 20, (remember, these are issues that were not being dealt with, essentially suppressed):

- Anger
- Self-esteem
- Lack of parental guidance

What I learned from professionals, Deanna's coaching, and life experiences:

- Emotional auras have the ability to impact those around us and I have learned to be cognizant of my own
- To open up and not be afraid to show or give love – personally, I will do my best to "end the (negative) family cycle."
- Being a "CWS" person was/is not an option

- To not let anger control me
- Anger masks hurt and fear
- Teaching from a parental perspective was not directed to me, I learned from "catching" and observing others along the way

Things to Consider:

Write down the positive and negative traits and characteristics from your parents. Write down any fears and or hurts from your childhood. Write down anything or event(s) (markers) from childhood that has negatively affected your life either in the past or current. What should you do to heal from your past. If you cannot resolve your issues on your own, have you considered professional counseling? Give yourself permission to change.

Notes and Affirmations:

_____

_____

_____

_____

_____

_____

_____

"Anger is like cancer. It eats upon the host.
But anger is like fire. It burns clean." - Maya Angelou

Deanna's Igniting Insights

As a career coach, I've learned and applied the fact that to create the life and vocation you are truly purposed to enjoy, it is an 85% inward thinking and only 15% application process. I learned that fact from my mentor, and author of "48 Days To The Work You Love", Dan Miller. It starts with how you (and others) label yourself. What is your identity? Who, or what experiences, do you attribute to your title(s)? Perhaps, some of these titles resonate with you: "Father/Mother", "Teacher", "Manager", "College Student", "Business Owner", etc. Sometimes, we allow negative labels to dictate who we believe we are, like: "Uneducated", "Unattractive", "Overweight", "Lonely", "Defeated", "Lost", "Tired", "Old", "Unworthy"...you see where this is going.

Now, we have all adjectives, no more nouns, to describe our title. Let's try it again. Who are you? Or, better yet, who do you aspire to be? If you are not a Christian, this doesn't apply, but if you are, our first identity or title would be "His Beloved Who Loves Jesus". Who do I aspire to be? Personally, I want to meet the Deanna who God originally authored, not the one born with sin and molded by the world for the past 52 years. A favorite affirmation is: "To the world, I am one, but to one, I am the world!" Whether you are a believer or not, this is true for all of us!

Let's look at how your title has changed throughout your life. When you were growing up, what did your 8-, 10-, or 15-year-old self *believe* you were going to be when you grew up? It is always so interesting to hear the results of this question. Most baby boomers seem almost embarrassed to answer, or they have to think awhile to realize what it was. Either that, or when they were a child, they hadn't experienced enough "worldly" influence for the dreams to be shattered, altered, or crushed.

People in today's workforce who are under-employed, unhappily employed, or unemployed can be traced back to allowing their destined title to be influenced negatively. It is a harsh fact we give permission to believe those things that are less than what our true purpose in life dictates. Typically, the initial consultation I have with clients reveals negative thoughts they *allowed* to take over what I call "mindshare". It's the "Coulda, Woulda, Shoulda" party Max discussed earlier.

I find when your thought process is occupied by more than 20% of negative influence, an overhaul is required. Sadly, the majority of those in later stages of life who have not encountered their lives' purpose are occupying their mindshare with more than 70% of negative thoughts about themselves and their accomplishments.

So, **Step One**: Assess what part of your "mindshare" is occupied with titles for yourself that are not becoming to what you aspire to be? Let's ask the question again: When you were young, what did you want to be when you grew up? No matter how *silly* you think it was/is, or how *unlikely* you think you can act on it now (negative mindshare), what is it you have missed out on for the over 30 years of adulthood? Do you know what is worse than 30 years of not doing what you were born to do? 30 years and one more day!

Give yourself permission to look into this further and really dig deeper into your childhood dreams. Often, they are in close proximity to your true purpose in life. I have found the detours from the aspirations of your youth (what you dreamed about becoming when you were younger) can often be found in our culture and with "well-intended" influencers in our life.

Perhaps, a parent said something similar to "You don't want to be a teacher. They don't make a lot of money." Or, women "Over 50" today were likely to hear something like, "Sweetheart, lawyers or doctors are really a man's domain. Perhaps you want to be a court reporter or nurse."

Then, there are the "not-so-well-intended" comments that are derived out of jealousy or just meanness: "You will never make it as a _____. Who do you think you are?" Or, "So, you think you are better than your parents? You think you *deserve* to be better than what you were born into?" And so on...

If those are similar to what you may have been told growing up, please allow me to bring truth to your being: You are designed to live a full and joyous life of giving and receiving, serving and being served, and loving and being loved. Read this paragraph again. Let the truth sink in. Breathe it in deeply.

Part of that equation is understanding what your purpose for a vocation is and running full and fast after it. One truth I remind people of often is this: If God placed a dream in your heart (which means it is good/wholesome), then He has already provisioned a path to achieve and live it! Even mistakes, failures, and detours serve the purpose of showing you how you may have gotten off-course.

My passion, which was realized later in life, is to help God's beloved (and everyone falls into this category) to find their true passion in life and help them with the process necessary to fulfill it. I absolutely love my "job" and believe with every fiber of my being everyone can find their true calling and be fulfilled in the way our Creator intended (which is much more than any of us could ever imagine) - no matter what stage in life they are in.

It takes *complete* transparency, *absolute* authenticity, and *genuine* faith.

Please note: I have not mentioned credentials, education, experience, or trade. It only takes passion. Passion capital, confidence, enthusiasm and likability are employable.

Step Two: Identify your passion - what is it that you could do all day, every day, even if you didn't get paid for it? Reminder: if you allow any negative thought to enter when you think about this, like, "I would love to fish every day, all day, *but I can't make a living at that.*", or, "I'd like to go golfing, however...", "I'd love to stay home with my grandchildren all day, but...", etc., I'd like you to give yourself permission (Yes, you are empowered to do that!) to ***forget*** all of the negative aspects, and imagine you could do what you loved *and* make a decent living at it.

What if every "job" paid $XXX,XXX (fill-in your desired amount) a year and you could engineer what it is that you *get* to wake up and do Monday – Friday? What would that be? What would your day, week, and month look like? What would you look like to those around you who you love when you completed the day doing what you loved to do?

Some of you knew immediately what it is that you wanted to do when you grew up; however, some of you are likely very perplexed right now and having a hard time absorbing what I'm asking/offering, which is the freedom to truly dream and know - without a doubt - what it is you were purposed to do/be. And, that's okay because we'll help you get there. I've personally helped many figure that out.

Now, I would recommend you take a personality profile assessment. I work with the DISC Personality Profile that gives you references to your personality, like who you would be most like in history, or what character in the Bible you would most be like. From there, we can quickly figure out what would NOT be a good fit, and then, carve out what would be a best fit for profession.

I often find us "Over 50's" have such low confidence in how to re-enter the workforce again, and, often, we focus on negative thoughts. I encourage you to be **completely uninhibited** in this process and imagine every negative obstacle you bring up can be knocked out easily...because it can.

If you fall into the category I previously mentioned (20-70% "mindshare" consumed with negative content, "CWS", or have any thoughts that are about your "history" and not your future), I want to challenge you with an exercise for assessment: Take a physical inventory of *every* thought and categorize it as being positive or negative. After a day, you will have quite a bit of content to apply the math.

If you discover you have the majority of thinking in the negative or historical category, then do this: Set aside a time of the day when you give yourself "permission" to reminisce about the past - only 10 minutes a day to have what I call an "Eeyore" party (from "Winnie The Pooh"), then all the other times of the day, when these negative thoughts are raised, give yourself "permission" to postpone them until your "Eeyore" appointment time.

As time goes by, you will find the time spent in negative condemnation is costing you joy, fulfillment, and purpose, not to mention what it may be costing you in your close relationships. I would challenge you to come up with the value of what those thoughts are costing you - not only in monetary value, but also relationship value (priceless!) as well.

Once you have knowledge of the true value of these negative thoughts, and refuse to allow them to *steal* from you anymore, you will resume a healthy thought process and start to come alive again in having "abundant mindshare" to learn new things and dream new dreams. Don't be discouraged if it takes some time and practice to change. Remember, you didn't acquire this condition overnight.

Here are some catchy "titles" I've used for myself and clients:

    Director of First Impressions
    Chief Inspiration Officer
    Client Success Manager
    Passion Interpretation Expert
    Career Transformation Expert
    CEO of Creativity

CHAPTER THREE

Behaviors and Influences
We Know-It-All Years

    Anger and fear go hand-in-hand, invisible co-conspirators and robbers of passion and dreams. My father's anger seemed to overshadow so much of my youth. And, this imprint not only impacted me, but my siblings as well. I recall being an angry teen, but when my father's anger and rage, for whatever the incident or infraction, manifested into a contorted facial expression, that was terrifying to me. It fueled fear and my own anger. While a more rational part of me tried to understand what was truly inciting his anger, it was still impossible not to react with my own anger and fear.

    Perhaps my father's anger was truly rooted in feelings of discrimination, or his own unfulfilled dreams, or worry about providing for a large family, feeling he was deprived of a formal secondary education, or general oppression. Who really knows? It could have been any, or all, of these things. But, instead of working through them or learning how to deal with them, they were expressed as frequent states of rage, taken out on my siblings and me.

Anger is a strong feeling of annoyance, displeasure or hostility. Synonyms include:

- Rage
- Vexation
- Exasperation
- Displeasure
- Irritation, irritability
- Indignation, pique

Fear is an unpleasant emotion caused by the belief someone or something is dangerous, likely to cause pain, or a threat. As a child, my daily existence seemed to be centered around, or dealing with, anger from my father and other "CWS" adults. In my experience, a typical adult conversation was centered on fear-based subject matter. Constantly judging others and the world while pointing the finger at others instead of objectively analyzing their own issues, problems, and failings. I think people find comfort in creating, or finding, fault in others it makes them feel better about themselves.

I identified my God-given talents, athletic ability, public-speaking, and intuition; however, I had no clue as to how to develop them. Fortunately, I learned early in life no matter my mistakes, errors, and shortcomings, as long as I tried and put forth the effort, the universe would send a person (or people) to help me to the next step. Always moving forward, always doing my best, always striving to be better than before. For every person or obstacle who/that came my way, the universe provided a person or situation to offer a solution, a path, a WAY!

In high school, I was a gifted track-and-field athlete, and, to this day, I believe my 1974 long jump record of 23 feet, 8 inches still stands. While I was a talented competitor, I was a poor student - not a good combination for college prep. In my senior year of high school, I had two car accidents. I crashed - and totaled - my Dad's '62 Chevrolet and, later, my own car that I worked so hard for and purchased with my money. When I crashed my dad's car at age 16, on a Friday, I went out of town to my friend's brother's house for the weekend. I was scared to death to go home and face my father's wrath! I strategically planned my return home for late Sunday afternoon, (supper-time) when my father would be in a *good mood*. Turned out to be a great move! ☺ When I walked in the door, my family looked at me with smiles and grins, as if they knew of my plan. I laughed along with them and proceeded to join in the buffet style supper. My father both glared and smiled at me simultaneously, while jokingly speaking of my poor driving skills.

I had both a healthy respect and unhealthy fear of my father. Healthy in the aspect of respecting him as every child should respect a parent, and unhealthy in the aspect I never felt like I could really talk to him about my challenges of puberty and becoming a man. These teachings would be left to observing my older brothers, uncles, and other, non-family male acquaintances.

My mother would talk to me and provide comfort when I needed it; however, I usually initiated the interaction. As a boy, I loved to put my head on her lap while she gently stroked my head. I was Mother's go to resource for family and household chores, like painting, mowing the yard, and gardening. She especially had a knack for home decorating. Even though she had no formal decorating training, it was natural instinct and talent for color and good taste. For holidays, especially Christmas, she had a list of household decorating things for me to work on, such as painting walls and trim.

I got a sense of responsibility and accomplishment from performing those duties, especially the creative value and the incentive of seeing the finished product. The true reward was when my family provided positive feedback and welcomed praises. I started mowing yards and raking leaves at the age of five to make money to buy candy, clothes, and the occasional gift for my mother.

My Uncle Ken was our neighbor. He lived next door with my other uncle, aunt and cousin. He was a young man, very intellectual, loved Jazz music, and dressed well. From ages five to nine or so, I spent more time with him than my own parents. He was responsible for giving me my nickname "Max", telling my mother I was no "Anthony", my given name.

In those days, there was a cartoon character named "Mack the Knife". Uncle Ken told my mother I was "sharp as a knife", but instead of calling me "Mack", he called me "Max" the Knife. So, "Max" has stuck with me for over 50 years. While my middle name is Steven and some family members still refer to me as "Stevie", "Max" is my best known name *and* the name I prefer.

Uncle Ken exposed me to several firsts in my boyhood: The name "Max", my first drive-in and indoor movies, he took me to the city of Winston-Salem, NC for the first time, which seemed so big in comparison to my hometown. Uncle Ken saw that "something special" in me. I was his sidekick, and he was my mentor, one of my role models and most influential people in my youth.

He died from a heart attack at the young age of 38 when I was only 9 years old. The transition of relational death or loss is very difficult to process as a child - the finality of never seeing or speaking to that person again in life. At a subconscious level, I thought his absence was temporary. I longed to see my uncle again, hoping one day to see him sitting in his green Chevrolet, and the nightmare of this loss finally over. But, he didn't return. I began to understand that life and people are not forever. In youth, we recover and move on quickly.

To this day, I think of Uncle Ken as my guardian angel. At a time when I felt alone and adrift, seeking love and attention from my parents, he was there to fill the void, to bring a much-needed spark to my life. Although Uncle Ken never married or had children of his own, I believe he loved me as the son he never had. Later in life, my experiences of relational death and loss took even a greater toll. Why? Because, in my 40's and 50's, I had many more years of life's experiences of living, loving, and caring.

My relationship with my Uncle Ken was so rewarding that I would often hang around adults. And, they enjoyed having me around because I was very mannerly, respectful, and inquisitive. I have sometimes been referred to as having an old soul. As a kid, I enjoyed listening to adult conversations and tried to understand their meaning. I felt my own age group had little to offer me in the way of learning or growth. Even to this day, in my 50's, many of my most insightful conversations are with people of senior age.

I was probably around 12 years old when I started to question the validity of a sixth sense. For me, it was intuition, the ability to understand something immediately, without the need for conscious reasoning, I felt my intuition was developing, along with a keen awareness of my environment and the people around me.

While my peer group focused on the "what" of life, I focused on the "why" and "how", which led me to critical thinking as a platform rather than a surface "what"-based analysis. It was fun to take a thought process from A to Z and predict each step in between.

It was particularly fun to watch a ball game (basketball, baseball, football, etc.) and try to predict the next play or event. I liked to anticipate a teacher's questions during class and the probability she would call on me to answer a question. The most fun was reading people, anticipating their needs and wants, and knowing if something was wrong.

Many times during my adolescence and young adulthood, people would comment about "the light in my eyes". Whatever the "something special" they were referring to me as a child, I now know, as an adult, to be a gift. Some may even say "IT"! But, the "IT", whatever that is, can only be given by a divine source.

As a child, I learned to use intuition to anticipate people and their actions. I never viewed it as an anomaly, only as an analytical focus and process. My "IT" was also charisma - I have been characterized as being charismatic by others all of my life. I suppressed my "IT" most of my adult life because I viewed charisma as negative, narcissistic, or ego. Only well into my 50's did I understand charisma to be a positive characteristic if used as such.

In school, I wasn't academically focused or prepared, and actually, I found school to be boring and a waste of time. I think this was primarily because education and academics were not focused on at home as important and fundamental aspects of life. My parents were organically intelligent, innovative, out-of-the-box thinkers. Today, they would likely have the opportunity to pursue and achieve all their goals and dreams. I got my "IT" and gift from a divine source. I have always tried to focus on doing good things with my life to honor them. While the seed of anger was passed down from my parents to me, but so were many positive talents and gifts.

My adolescent role models were family, Uncle Ken, brother "Chip", Muhammad Ali, James Bond, Martin Luther King, Jr., John F Kennedy, school teachers, and entertainers like Cary Grant and Sean Connery. These people left an imprint on me. Some inspired me, some I aspired to be, some I admired and wished to emulate, some were the cultural environment that was representative of my youth. I took something positive from each one, learning and evolving along the way. The following were my takeaways at this time:

Family: My seven older brothers and sisters - I looked up to them as adults and mentors. My younger brother was viewed as the "baby" of the family.

Uncle Ken: He loved me and spent time with me. He was one of my mentors and a friend. He saw something special in me and made me feel relevant. I will always love him.

"Chip": He was my brother, approximately 10 years older than I. He went into the Navy in the early 1960's and traveled the world during his 20-plus-year career. He was the first and only one of my siblings to leave home and start a career abroad. I looked up to him as a role model that I could emulate - if he could do it, so could I!

Martin Luther King, Jr.: Civil Rights Leader and Nobel Prize Winner. His oratory skills and confidence led me to public speaking. There are people who are positioned and groomed for pivotal leadership positions in history, when society and the world need them most. He was one of those people in the 1960's.

John F. Kennedy: Thirty-fifth President of the United States of America. The Cuban Missile Crisis of 1962 was a frightening time for Americans, and I can recall people rushing to the grocery stores and emptying shelves in preparation of potential nuclear disaster. I was only 6 years old but can still vividly recall the fear within my own family. Watching President Kennedy on black-and-white television has been etched into my memory of what a leader and leadership should look like: Firm and unyielding yet diplomatic, determined and clear yet flexible, and comfortable in setting proper expectations for outcomes. Young, handsome, and articulate, his eloquent rhetoric also planted the seed of public speaking into my psyche.

Muhammad Ali: A man of conviction, principle, and character. He was the most revered, respected, and admired athlete of my youth. I wanted to emulate his authenticity, dignity, courage, and love for people.

Sean Connery "007": "James Bond" was a movie screen icon in the 1960's. Sophisticated, worldly, handsome, charismatic, world traveler, and filled with passion to save the world from evil villains. It didn't hurt he was always surrounded by beautiful women. As a kid, I saw my brother, "Chip", as our "James Bond".

Cary Grant: As a Hollywood actor, he was the consummate performer and a lady's man of the 1950's and 1960's. His demeanor, style, and dress were captivating with a smooth, distinguished voice and a British accent.

Motown: The artists and music of Motown in the 1960's were the most important social dynamics to bring black and white cultures together, both as listeners and participants in the "cooling" of America! Jazz music began the "cooling" culture process in the 1940's. Then, Motown took it to another level in the 1960's.

My Father: He was totally focused on physical health and fitness. I think it was his way of channeling his anger and releasing it through exercise. To this day, it is this single virtue of exercise which provided (and still provides) holistic transformation when I need it most.

My Mother: Ultimately, my mother, who constantly worked hard doing the cooking, cleaning, and maintaining of our large family, was one of the most influential role models in my life for the following reasons: She was my first love, kind-hearted, gentle, intelligent, comforting, religious, courageous, and strong-willed. She also had high integrity and an enormous work ethic. She was the disciplinarian who raised 9 children with very little money...and, she totally started her life over in her 50's with passion and zeal! She lived to be 81 years old. Amazingly, I knew her for 39 years and only saw her angry once, maybe twice - she was the most self-controlled person I've ever known.

These people were both directly and indirectly influences on me because I saw and felt something in them I wanted to emulate in my own life. During these years, I learned to question the "why" of life. That was far more interesting than the "what" of life. For me, "why" always answered the "what" because "why" is analysis and "what" is situation-specific. Every human being, at some point, ponders these life's questions for individual reasons.

"What" versus "Why"?

    What is going on?
    Why is it going on?

    What is the matter with you?
    Why are you behaving this way?

    What do you want?
    Why do you want it?

    What happened?
    Why did it happen?

One must think deeper to ponder the "why" of anything. It takes effort, time, and both *objective* and *subjective* thinking for answers to things that matter. The psychological and emotional imprints of our youth provide identifiable reasons why we do (or do not) perform certain behaviors.

As a minority student at my high school of approximately 1,500 students, I decided to run for Senior Class President against an all-white field of contenders. All candidates had to give our "stump" speech to the entire student body. I heard around school that most students believed I couldn't win! Why? I was African-American *and* poor running against the school's white academic and socio economic elite.

Yes, a win was unlikely, but I dug in and created my "stump" speech, practicing it over and over again. The day of the speech delivery finally arrived. I was prepared yet nervous. When my turn came to speak, I stood proudly, masking my nervousness, and delivered a resounding and passionate speech which was organized, clearly outlining goals for my presidency.

Afterwards, numerous students and teachers approached me with congratulatory sentiments. Evidently, I surprised many while making a positive impact with both students and faculty alike. My younger brother, Sam, attended and was "blown away" by my presentation.

It was my first time on stage as a public speaker...and Sam's first time to see me as such. I felt like I was 10 feet tall! Even the accolades for my track-and-field accomplishments paled in comparison to my first academic and social achievement.

Ultimately, I came in second and was elected as the Student Body Vice President. Obviously, I was still elated, especially since I did not expect to place at all. And, from this experience, I learned to use others' negative, or low/no, expectations of me as motivation. To this day, I love it when people underestimate me - it fuels my passion to succeed. The imprint of "I'm good enough and as good as anyone else" had been set.

The primary industries of my small hometown were furniture and glass manufacturing and poultry production. In the 1960's and '70's, these labor jobs were plentiful, and demand was high. I worked at the poultry plant twice and the furniture factory once during high school to earn enough money to purchase my first car and school clothes, as well as having some spending money. I viewed these jobs as a *temporary* means to achieve short-term goals, save for college, and leave my community.

My father had an entirely different perspective. He believed you get a job and keep it forever. I never understood his rationale since he had always maintained his own auto repair business. I think, on a subconscious level at least, he resented the prospects of his children becoming educated and pursuing more professional careers - something he had not achieved himself.

Some parents work and plan for their children to become more and do better in life than themselves. Sadly, others seem to suppress and block advancement because it's too painful to look at themselves in the mirror.

My father's generation, born in the early twentieth century, could be regimented, cold, and callous people (at least not outwardly affectionate), not necessarily because it was their inherent character, but, rather, learned behaviors based upon experiences and imprints. My father would constantly say to me, "Get a job at the poultry plant, and work your way up to supervisor." I rebelled against the very notion of limiting my vision and goals to becoming a laborer at a factory for the rest of my life. There's nothing wrong with being a worker in a plant, but it was not for me; I had other plans.

How and why did the seeds of anger manifest in me as a young man? I have sought out psychological counseling on at least three occasions in my life - twice for depression and once for divorce. I'm a big advocate of seeking professional help and counsel for psychological and emotional health matters.

However, in those days, people relied on "old school" therapies and home remedies, God, and church. Most people could neither afford nor understand the need for professional counseling. It was a "taboo" subject, especially in the African-American community. The environment to which we're born and raised has a significant impact on how we view the world and how we determine our behavioral benchmarks.

My father's anger along with his aloofness and lack of ability to display outward emotion and love to his children were traits that, at the time, I believed to be the way the male head of the household was supposed to behave. While I assumed this was standard behavior, I resented it and vowed this would not be the way I would deal with fatherhood.

As we live, we learn, understand, and start to piece together the puzzle pieces of our lives. The anger I had as a young adult was generated by environment, people, situations, and society in the following ways:

- Observing the example of my father
- Lack of (visible) love from my parents
- Lack of (obvious) guidance
- Low self-esteem
- People can be selfish
- Trust issues
- Discrimination
- Constant and consistent "mantras" that went against my aspirations, goals, and dreams

One of my quests later in life was to understand why I was so angry and how to come to terms with this emotion (and its resulting behaviors) and learn to end it. Life is a great teacher, and I eventually would gain understanding and find true, lasting peace.

What about you? Are there people or experiences from your youth that created an issue or repressed complex that caused psychological conflict? If yes, then know you're not alone.

My beach ball challenges and issues, age 20 to 30:

- Fear
- Anger
- Career
- Passions
- Dreams
- Lack of Self-love
- Low Self-esteem
- Understanding and cultivating my "IT"

What I Learned about Anger, Fear, and Role Models:

- Anger is "quicksand"
- Everyone has "beach ball" experiences
- Live a curious and inquisitive life
- Don't blame others for your problems
- End the cycle of anger and fear with my own family
- Fear is a robber of passion and personal growth

- Negative imprints can last forever if not diagnosed and addressed
- To know your "why" can create passion or depression - it's a matter of choice
- The "why" of my life has changed as I have over time
- Role models and people who inspire you help to mold and shape your character

Notes and Affirmations:

_____
_____
_____
_____
_____
_____
_____
_____
_____
_____
_____

Deanna's Beach Ball Deep Dive

Everyone inherits what I call "traditional sin", or generational ways. Those biases, abusiveness, and negative or uneducated traits passed on to us from our parents, grandparents, close friends, and extended family. In addition, there are "cultural sins" and traditions that are derived from where (or when) we grew up, or perhaps, where we worked for an extended period of time.

For me, and perhaps some of you, I always considered myself to be "a good person". If I offended someone by what I did or said it was not "intentional". I shudder to think how many of my youthful ignorance's and generational sins affected others.

Today, I want more than just to be a good person, I want to make significant positive impact in others' lives and intentionally be known to be relentlessly kind. I want to tell everyone I know about Jesus - without using any words! I know I will fall short, but I aim high.

It wasn't until I developed an "all-in" mindset and heart to run fast and hard after the relationship I have with Jesus that His true character started taking up residence in my heart and mind. Subsequently, he showed (and shows) me my many shortfalls and traditional ways that are not reflective of who He wants me to be. And most importantly, how someone that represents (and claims to know) Him should be acting and thinking. Sometimes, in certain situations or relationships, all we can come up with is "something just isn't right". When I experience this, there is only one source for reference and clarity; God's word! Followed by the action plan of prayer and ultimately the voice of the Holy Spirit confirming direction and resolving the conflict.

There are positive influences in our lives and inevitable negative influences. Why do we feel it mandatory to continue with some that are negative? Could it be because of traditional ways? For example, what if it is your family that are pouring into you the behaviors that are not becoming to who you aspire to be? That's a tough one, but ultimately, we are called to love. We can extend kindness, forgiveness and love without joining in on bad behaviors.

In order to arm ourselves with the skills and action plans we need to gracefully conquer the transitions that come along later in life, we need to take inventory of where and what source we draw from.

Make a list of the people in your life that you spend the most time with, sort them from most to least time spent. Now, ask yourself if you are spending the most time with your most favorite and admired person. The one that challenges you to be a better you. Next, organize another list and place the order in the people you most *want* to spend time with, again those that will inspire, admire, encourage and uplift. If your most favored is not at the top, (after Jesus of course), then, if at all possible, make it a priority to spend more and most of your time with them. We can and will get through these challenges in life, but we don't have to make it harder on ourselves by taking the journey alone.

Something that just touched my heart is that someone reading this may have lost their 'favorite' and 'beloved' name on the top of both lists. I am truly sorry if you are hurting. There is only one source that knows your pain and that is our Creator. Ask Him to surround you with His love, strength, sustainability and comfort that only He can deliver. Then ask Him to fill the emptiness that may exist with joy and hope once again. Believe that if there is breath in your lungs, then you, my friend, have a purpose. Ask Him to reveal it to you.

Anger and fear negatively affects our forward progress to live out our dreams and passions. At some point, as we know better, we should do and be better. Like Max's past, there could be seeds in you that you have not dealt with.

The beach ball effect is a metaphor that represents all of our things in life that we haven't dealt with.

Here are just some examples of what fills our beach ball:

- Regret
- Not forgiving others
- Postponement of anything that would improve our lives or others
- Not taking time to grieve
- Avoidable health issues

- Lack of financial planning
- Not planning for empty nesting
- Keeping a job you hate

The beach ball effect references the outcome of snoozing what is filling the ball, and the result is like holding a beach ball underwater. The challenge to balance the weight and buoyancy of the beach ball, the strength and energy consumed by the act of holding it down.

When we postpone, ignore, or refuse to acknowledge issues arising in our lives and relationships - I imagine these things to manifest into filling several beach balls full of air and juggling trying to keep them under water. The more we have, the more energy, time and strength it takes to manage them. Think of it like a snooze button in our life, however the more we push the snooze button on issues, or dreams, or forgiveness for instance, the more air is pumped in our beach balls, making it harder and harder to keep under water. Eventually, these balls will pop up to the surface, typically at the most inopportune time and often "hitting" or affecting those that are closest to us.

If that is the case for you, seek wise counsel and begin to develop the knowledge and skills you need to manage your way through them – know that your authentic joy and happiness is patiently waiting for you to let go of the snooze buttons in life and release the beach ball!

CHAPTER FOUR

*Keep Moving Forward
Clear But Not*

"Be careful what you wish for, you just might get it." - Anonymous

In my senior year of high school, my primary focus was on three things: 1.) Getting an athletic scholarship in track-and-field, 2.) Graduating high school, and 3.) Going to college. My backup plan, if I did not get a scholarship and go away to college, was to work part-time and attend community college. Then, ultimately, I would leave my hometown for a big-time university, or at least go to work in some big city.

Without the socio-economic advantages the middle class and upper middle class students in my high school had, I felt disheartened. I only had myself, my athletic ability, a likeable personality, and a dream of becoming someone and doing something in life. But, life is not fair - growing up black *and* poor in America was (and still is) a double set of hurdles to navigate.

It was in my senior year that I acknowledged my God-given gift for oratorical skills in public speaking. My first presentation campaigning for Student Body Class President emboldened me to compete in the Kiwanis Club State Oratory contest. I came in third place, and, in hindsight, had I prepared better, I believe I would have won. Also, at this time, I realized I had two additional attributes: 1) Determination and 2) Resilience. The two most enduring qualities of survival - I would certainly need these as underpinning for my life's journey.

The accolades I received for my oratory skills boosted some of my self-esteem and gave me the courage to ask out a girl in my neighborhood I always liked, but lacked the confidence to approach. When she said yes, I was thrilled with her (and myself). I introduced Jenny to my mother, and Mother immediately liked her. Jenny was the only girl I brought home who Mother liked and approved of. My confidence and self-esteem were definitely improving. I continued to excel in competitive track-and-field events and colleges and universities were taking notice. Scholarship offers were starting to come in. Life was good!

When I was 17, things looked promising. Then, suddenly, Jenny tells me she's pregnant! My world seemed to shatter. I didn't have the financial resources to support a family, my GPA was not good, and my SAT scores were barely marginal. My grades were so bad, I did not know if I would graduate until a few days before the actual graduation ceremony. It was only one class - history - that would determine whether I would receive my diploma or not. Then, to my relief and joy, I got the passing grade. To this day, I believe it was the mercy of my history teacher and my guardian angel, Uncle Ken, who helped get me through this and get my high school diploma.

I relied on athletic ability, rather than academics, as the key to going to college. Had I applied myself academically I could have been a high achiever. That's the importance of having value on education taught and exemplified by parents.

I was elated to graduate high school and achieve the first of my three primary goals. My second and third goals were coming to fruition when I verbally accepted a scholarship award from a college in Tennessee. This was even more exciting as it also meant I would get to move away from my home town and escape the dark cloud that life in my hometown seemed to represent. The university scholarship was contingent upon my final SAT scores. Optimistically, I planned for my future, which was I would work hard over the summer, save money, go off to college for a year, then bring Jenny and our baby back to Tennessee.

The big day finally arrived for me to leave for college. My brother, Chip, was visiting home from the Navy and drove me to Tennessee since he was heading to a Navy base there. It was a day of both joy and sadness - the joy of leaving my hometown and going to college, and the sadness of leaving

Jenny, my unborn child, and my mother. It was so fitting my brother, who was one of my major role models, took me to college that day.

When we arrived at the university, I was absolutely blown away by the grandeur of the buildings, manicured lawns, and the euphoria of going off to college. We went to the track coach's office, and he gave us the campus tour, including the track-and-field stadium. My dream had come true, or at least partially true.

After the tour, he escorted me to what would be my dorm room. Because he had an appointment, he asked me to come to his office later. When I arrived there, I thought we would be discussing Freshman Orientation and our next steps for meeting the other athletes.

However, his demeanor was serious and apologetic. I sat down, and he proceeded to say the words that would change my life forever, "Max, we just received your SAT scores, and they are not high enough to allow you entry to the university. I'm sorry."

At first, I thought it was a joke, but, after he exhaled, I clearly understood it to be reality. In the span of approximately one hour, I went from one of the "highest highs" of my life to the "lowest ebb." I wanted to die! But then, he proceeded to tell me there was another university near Nashville, Tennessee that would accept me with full scholarship.

Chip picked me up and drove me to the other university. I was, eighteen, with a child on the way, humiliated things did not work out with the university I wanted to attend. At this point, my future seemed so uncertain. But, *I kept moving forward.*

I realized early on that life is filled with transitions, challenges, ups and downs. The only way to stay down or "stuck" is to give up, and giving up is not in my nature. Every step forward opened new doors and opportunity. After a year with good scholastic transcripts, I could have transferred back to my original university choice.

My brother did all he could to help me, both with moral and financial support. At that time, he was the only person in my life who showed me he cared. During this period of feeling dejected, alone, and isolated, I started to grow up as a man, block out the naysayers, and believe in myself. As determination and resilience were kicking in, I also sensed someone or something was looking out for and guiding me. My inner voice was telling me to take the hits and blows, stay focused and positive, embrace change, and everything will work out. It did and has always done so throughout my life.

I stayed for five or six weeks at the second university, then left to visit Jenny and my new son who had just been born back in North Carolina. I missed physically being there for his birth, but made a vow to become a great dad.

My plan was to stay for a week, then return to school, and prepare for Jenny and my son to be with me within a matter of months. It did not work out that way. When I saw my son for the first time with his mother, I knew I could not return to school. I was 18 years old, bent but not broken, bewildered but determined to somehow move forward.

I just did not know where and how things would work, but, again, resilience and determination kept me moving forward. I ended up getting a job as a janitor (night gig) at the same high school where, just months earlier, I had been Student Council VP, and track star. Fortunately, it was a graveyard shift, so none of the students who knew me would ever see me as what they would likely surmise as an 18-year-old failure. But, I wasn't a loser or failure - I was a winner who kept moving forward. Jenny and I got married, not really knowing what the future held.

Then, I joined the Army National Guard, where I excelled in Army Basic Training and even was asked if I was interested in joining the Green Beret, or perhaps pursuing a military career via a West Point education. The Army Cadre saw my potential for leadership and gave me the opportunity to write my own ticket.

Great, right? But, I wasn't interested in the military as a career, and after three or four months, I asked for, and received, an Honorable Discharge based upon my family needs. I wanted to work in Corporate America. I felt my core skills for leadership and the ability to communicate would be better served in the private sector.

I had no regrets with my decision because I was focused on building a great life for my family, and being a positive example for my child. The Army National Guard was a great experience, and huge esteem builder - they saw potential in me, and that felt good! This endorsement of the National Guard of my skills, as well as, being a young dad and husband were impactful events that initiated my journey from young country boy to responsible man.

Now, at this point, I'm nineteen, back home in North Carolina, married with a son, and no job. But, I'm determined to get back into college, run track, and take care of my family. No matter the challenges my family and I face, we were moving forward. No matter how hard being in my hometown seemed to feel like my dreams were being smothered, I was going to get my family out of that environment.

I still had major colleges and universities interested in my athletic talents; however, my SAT scores were holding me back. So, I enrolled in a junior college in Virginia and took my family with me. My wife and I worked several jobs while I was in college full-time, and we had a good life.

I stayed at the junior college where I did not complete the Associate Degree program. After Virginia, I was destined to move in a westerly direction - first to Texas, then, on to California. I came from a small town and knew the kind of prospects for career advancement and personal growth I wanted could only be found in a major city. I wanted more opportunity and prospects for a career than what Virginia had to offer in the mid-70's.

Houston, Texas was where I dropped anchor. My wife and family were supportive, and so we went for it! So, we moved to Texas, where my younger brother was enrolled on a full track-and-field scholarship at a Houston university.

Moving to a large city was not an easy transition. The contrast between my small hometown and this very large city was a journey in uncharted and unknown territory for my family and me, but I was determined to move forward for growth, opportunity and happiness. Houston, Texas would be one of the best decisions that I ever made for me and my family, quality of life, career, and opportunity. No risk, no reward.

My goals were to get a job, enroll in college, get an apartment, and bring my wife and son out to be with me, where we could live as a family. I worked several jobs, slept on my brother's dorm room floor, and saved money. My son and wife stayed with her mother in North Carolina, while I found employment and housing. I did not go back to college because, ultimately, I had a family and needed to make enough money to support us all. If a college degree was in my future, I would make it happen, determined to be successful with or without a degree, I was confident in my possibilities for success, I just did not know how it would happen. I relied on faith, intelligence, "common sense", a developing vision and a willingness to fail my way forward. My focus was on intellect, talent, skill and know-how above physical athletic ability.

In the 70's there were no peer pressure problems, or emotional issues that I tried to medicate with drugs, I experimented just a fun thing, seeking new state-of-mind experiences, and because it was the era of the hippie movement and counter culture, that most people in my age group did back in the 70's. Back then, hippies created their own communities, listened to psychedelic music, embraced the sexual revolution, and used drugs to explore altered states of consciousness. I feel no inhibition about writing this because it's the truth, and I'm not running for political office. If you're "Over 50", then you may relate to the memory of that era.

Back in the early '80's, affirmative action, which was designed to redress the disadvantages associated with past (and present) discrimination of racial minorities and women, benefitted me in obtaining my first, professional-level job in Corporate America. I was 26-years-old. My starting salary as a Computer Account Executive was $22,500, not bad in 1983.

This was during the advent of and introduction to the Personal Computer (PC). I worked for a technical equipment provider, the world's largest manufacturer of mid-range server computers and systems. They generated more than $25B in annual revenues with more than 40k employees worldwide. My job was to sell PCs to commercial and oil and gas business customers.

Within a few years, I was promoted to Business Account Manager, selling large computer systems to big, multi-national accounts, in the oil and gas field, as well as aerospace and technology fields, and others in the vast industrial market.

I loved sales. The natural art and science of selling products and services came easy to me, and I worked very hard to hone my skills and talents. "Sales" was natural and comfortable for me. My oratory skills were an asset in my sales capacity along with my determination and resilience. I enjoyed dressing professionally and working with high-ranking individuals and companies in Corporate America.

I felt a great debt of gratitude for the people responsible for hiring me. They saw desire, passion, and perseverance in me, and I was determined not to let them down. Here, I was coming into my own as a man and professional, clearly defining and understanding the four pillars of my being:

1. Passion
2. Risk
3. Challenge
4. Resilience

Passion is the fuel for dreams, and I had it in abundance. My passion for sales was endless, and I was eager to be the best sales professional possible. I believed "sales" was a calling because it was who I was as a person. I could naturally read people and situations, orchestrate and manage resources, and execute strategic business plans that won multi-million dollar deals.

Risk means going to the edge and either building a bridge to the next step or stage or failing. The higher the risk, the higher the reward - this is a fair and reasonable equation. I lived on the business edge, took risk, then did whatever it took to win; and, more often than not, winning was the outcome.

Challenge makes us grow as human beings. Nothing is more satisfying than overcoming a challenge or obstacle, and each time we do it, we become stronger and stronger. When we maintain this mindset throughout life, by the time we're in our 50's, our ability to overcome life's challenges should become easier, not harder, because we know our individual formula for success and know that, no matter what, we will be okay.

Resilience over time makes you a diamond. Often, especially in midlife, the brilliance of our diamond's "bling" may dim or even be covered with life's "coal or mineral residue". It's never too late to buff and clean your diamond's essence back to its original luster and smooth out the rough edges. Consistent resilience - coupled with passion, taking risk, and overcoming challenges - becomes more important in life's second half than in the first half. The so-called "fountain of youth" flows from a life based on passion, constant personal growth, and development.

I consistently exceeded my sales objectives, and, within only a few years, had established a reputation for sales success and leadership. In 1986, after I had blown away sales objectives for three straight years and received President's Club awards, I was confident in my abilities and talents.

While I was successful based on my abilities, my eyes were being opened to the "Corporate America jungle." I began to see this "jungle" as a place and thing based upon survival of the fittest, in terms of office politics, and games of duality, and deceit. The canvas of my career life was becoming more *clear, but not.*

Old and Outdated Corporate Philosophy
- First In, Last Out - Old School "Crock"
    - Old School - Being the first into the office and the last one to leave, exhibits dedication and hard work. Sacrifice family time for the perception of dedication
    - New School - Work virtual from anywhere, perform, and get the work and job done. Balance between family and work
- Open Door is Open Policy
    - Old School - Open door is a "trap", unless you are a part of the crony network. Don't do it. The open door is only designed to filter out those who management thinks don't belong in the organization
    - New School - Usually don't stay with a company where "open door" would be needed. Move on to the next opportunity
- Perception is Reality
    - Another Old School "crock": If people are threatened by your performance or taking their job, they can easily create a perception that's a lie only to remove you as a threat. This practice is still in vogue today, just orchestrated in a different manner
    - New School - More open minded to alternative perceptions and views
- Never Leave a Job or Company Because of a "Bad Boss"
    - Old School - This was an unwritten rule all of my years in corporate. I have personally experienced situations where I would have been much happier had I left the job or company. No boss or job is worth prolonged unhealthy pain and stress
    - New School - Low to no tolerance or loyalty for a "boss" or crony. Loyalty to transparent leadership and fairness

Lessons learned from instincts, mentors, and coaching:

- Think positive
- Expect the best
- Question assumptions
- Seek out mentorship
- Be passionate about your work

- Learn all that you can, seek training
- Manage your direct hierarchy (Manager)
- Get all promises and negotiations in writing
- Seek out education programs, such as tuition reimbursement
- When wronged, use the least amount of force necessary
- Know your value, and do not accept anything less than you deserve
- Negotiate from a position of strength...**and** be willing to walk away from the table if needed

Things to Consider:

- If you're stuck and don't know what to do "Over 50", hire a Career Transition Coach
- Learn to be more adaptable to change and develop new perspectives
- Connect with Millennials for a novel exchange of vision, focus and ideas
- Reassess your definition of career and employment success
- Stay fresh! Retool talents and skills inventories for greater learning
- If you're unhappy with your job or career, define your value and non-negotiables, find a way to create passion in work so it's no longer work
- Take control of your career, with focus on performance and growth
- Law #1 - Whoever owns the company you work for can do whatever they want with the company and assets, including its employees within the law. Creating your own business is always an option. Whatever you decide to do, please do what you love.
- Law #2 - If you continue to work for someone else, a company, or yourself, every career move should be a move towards professional growth and freedom. Search for a company and culture that aligns with your core values.

"If work was so great, the rich would own It." - Mark Twain

Notes and Affirmations:

_____
_____
_____
_____
_____
_____

Deanna's Process to Propel Forward

I spent the first twenty-eight years of my career in job positions that were a polar-opposite match from my authentic personality. I was "performing" my way through most of my day. I remember learning there was a "process" to sales, where you didn't have to be natural at being a jerk to be successful (I'm sorry, but that was what I was brought up around and how I was taught - I was told it was an essential element to success).

I was able to follow the process, work longer and harder, and truly succeed. But, I was filling my work day with an Oscar-worthy performance. My personality was not cut out for cold-calling, rejection, fighting for better territories, or challenging co-workers over encroachments to my assigned accounts. Thank goodness I was able, however, to be authentic at home with family and friends.

While some folks actually choose a career that allows them to get away from their home life, I couldn't wait for holidays, and, especially, vacations. What's interesting now is I can relate, first-hand, to my clients when we identify a mismatch in careers to their personality type. Trust the timing of your life.

Now, don't get me wrong. We can be very good at what we do, perhaps even at the top of our game. But, if it is a day full of wishing we were elsewhere, what good does that do for living authentically to how you were made? We can be good at something and not love, or even like, it.

With that said, I made a lot of money in my mismatched profession of sales and sales management. My personality actually was cut-out for sales, at least in the long-term, relationship-building, and multi-purchases aspects of sales; however, once "promoted" to management (because of stellar performance), that's where it went off rails.

Why is it, in Corporate America, that the better you are at what you do, the tradition has been to promote you? Perhaps, you are reading this wondering if that is where it all went off course for you as well. At some point, the stress of performing your way through the majority of your day/week/year, etc. catches up to you, and, in the very least, makes you ponder the question I challenge you with now: What if you couldn't wait for

Monday? What if you didn't think of your job as a "job", but as "an outpouring prayer offering to an awesome, loving God"? When we are blessed to know our "calling" and able to live out our purpose, it is not work! It is the excitement and passion and, most importantly, *fulfillment* that comes from living your life freely and on purpose.

Are you imagining this for yourself? Are you juggling negative thoughts, like, "I don't deserve to…?" Well, if you are, reschedule all of that for your Eeyore appointment time, and let's get real with envisioning what that exciting, passionate, fulfilling life could look like for you. Here's the thing: I don't want to help you find employment; I want to help you find a vocation that you absolutely love to wake up every day and go and do - not perform - but **DO**!

Max had many surprises throughout his young adult life. Much of the plans he had been dreaming of and counting on for so many years came to a halt, due to some 'curve balls' and 'u-turns' he had to maneuver through. It all came down to him making decisions. Some decisions were right, others he may have chosen another route if he had it to do over. But, all of his choices involved deciding on a course of action and then moving forward.

Some of us get stuck in not knowing what to do, or are trapped, so upset by the circumstances, and we get paralyzed in fear and uncertainty. Making a decision to do anything is too overwhelming; we hit the snooze button again and again. I like to remind clients that doing nothing, in reality, is a decision; a bad one --- but it is one.

Even if the decision you make leads to unsuccessfulness (which I believe is temporary and God's purpose for you is yet to be revealed), at least you fail falling forward! Indecision is the greatest thief of opportunity! The wealthiest people have often failed many times prior to reaching their height of success. Thus, our failures bring us closer to our inevitable success.

Here is our starting point for moving forward: Write down your goals! If you have no goals, then get some! I cannot express how very important goal-setting and goal-documentation are - especially during these life transitions.

I've been a goal-setter for over 30 years. In my opinion, it is something you must acquire and be disciplined in to be successful, in sales particularly, but also in our personal lives.

I have read articles and heard only 3% of the population writes down their goals. So here, I'll reference a study about goal-setting from the Harvard MBA program. The study revealed that only 3% of students had written goals and plans to accomplish them; 13% had goals in their minds, but hadn't written them down; 84% of the students had no goals at all.

After 10 years, the 13% who had goals, but had not written them down made, on average, twice the amount of money than the 84% with no goals. Astonishingly though, the 3% who had written down their goals AND their plans on how to achieve them, made, on average, TEN TIMES as much income as the other 97%!

People who don't write down their goals tend to fail easier than the ones who have written plans. Who would want to sign up for something that encourages you to fail easier? By not writing down your goals, that is what you are signing up to do...fail easier. I've always heard, and truly believe, a goal written down is **90%** achieved. Talk about an easy way to begin forward motion!

In coaching job transition, one of the first things we map out is a date of which the client would want to be employed at a new job. From that date, we work backwards and determine what actions need to be done each day in order to have the very best chance of fulfilling the desired employment date. Then, the client has daily decisions to make. He/she can either complete the goals and tasks required that day, or *choose* to prolong employment for another day past the goal date.

It is forward motion actions and great planning that guarantee vast success! Whether you are transitioning from/to a new career or job, single life, empty nesting, grief recovery, or health and wellness, written goals with date-driven plans on how to accomplish them will propel you to your desired destination the fastest and most effective way!

I love to look back on my annual goals and see the results; it really is amazing! If you are not a goal-setter (yet), may I strongly encourage you to start today! You can start with just one, even if it's a small one. Get a taste for success. One year from now you will be most grateful you took the thought process and placed it to paper so you can look back and see the *tangible* benefits from written goals. Without a target, you have a 100% chance of missing your shot.

Even though Max had a lot of surprises throughout his life and many recalibrations of his goals and dreams, the good news is nothing was or is a surprise to God. He has had our days mapped out in each and every detail before we were even born. Tapping into our great Creator and gaining wisdom from Him as to what our purpose is or will be and how to set our goals from His perspective is the fastest route to our joy-filled destination

Here is where I encourage forward motion, *of any kind*. I call it "praying with your legs". It is amazing that once you start propelling in forward motion, you start accumulating small victories.

Those small victories turn into a trajectory of on-purpose actions, which ultimately lead to achieving your goals. You may not know what it is exactly you are going to do yet, but forward motion is still important.

Go to networking events, which reminds me of a client: When I told her to start attending networking events, she told me she was "socially constipated." Perhaps, not wanting to be associated with that title - "socially constipated" - will get you out there a little faster.

Volunteer. It is another powerful tool and can be framed on your résumé as to not have any gap in your employment. You can acquire transferrable skills and meet new people to network with. In addition, nothing compares to serving others when it comes to your self-worth and true joy. God wants us to be obsessively preoccupied with the needs of others.

Read books (in addition to the one you are reading now). Your DISC Personality Profile will outline weaknesses you may be prone to have. I recommend reading a book that will strengthen you in those areas (and you will be using that later when you prep for interviews). Any self-improvement book should lift your outlook and keep you up-to-date and relevant.

The power of accomplishment does one's self-confidence good. To be employable, one must be confident, enthusiastic, and likeable; *all* of these are fueled by genuine passion.

So, start your forward motion action plan today, or next Monday. Just keep in mind that "Someday" is not a day of the week.

CHAPTER FIVE

Career and Cronyism
"Smoke Screen"

As a young adult, my dream was to be an integral part of Corporate America. I envisioned tailored suits, a large office, with a huge, gleaming mahogany desk and a large, leather executive chair waiting for me. My vision included working and collaborating with respected, polished professionals and my contributions would be acknowledged and applauded; I was going to work hard to be the absolute best I can be and better than they anticipated.

Throughout my corporate career, I did realize my vision, and it felt great! I was a respected member of the corporate circle, achieving financial success. But, my journey took a turn, and it was not a good one. Not only did I add the meaning of the word 'cronyism' to my vocabulary, but I was thrust in the front row of corporate cronyism at its best, or perhaps, more appropriately, at its worst. Carefully orchestrated *"smokescreen"* designed to disguise and conceal real intentions and activities.

> Cronyism is "the unfair practice by a powerful person of giving jobs and other favors to friends."

It is unfortunate, but in my experience and the experience of numerous others I've known, cronyism has reared its ugly head at one time or another. Cronyism is not only a plague - it's become a pandemic! My 26 year old Nephew (CPA) is currently navigating the "Crony Waters" of a major corporation. He has shared with me that my Coaching, regarding awareness and travail of this business culture have been very accurate. Within his group, negative attitudes, declining performance, lack of enthusiasm, motivation and frustration have permeated.

In the definition of cronyism, the operative word is "unfair." If a person in power brings someone in who is qualified, adept, and has a successful track record, that person can add value to the team and the organization. However, if the only credential they have is being a friend or buddy to one in power, the dynamics of the team have been turned askew; the rest of the team is in an unfair situation. Morale, esteem, productivity and collaboration are compromised. (In the case of an unqualified family member being unfairly appointed to a lucrative position the correct term would be "nepotism".)

What ensues with cronyism is resentment and antagonism over what has been allowed to happen. I have seen cronyism taken to the next level, meaning the person in power who brought their crony into the organization has realized he's made an error. To deflect blame and create a perceived distance, their crony is promoted. This is a subterfuge technique and the process can be done repeatedly, ultimately wreaking havoc along the way.

This reminds me of a quote I once heard; "Never ascribe to malice that which is adequately explained by incompetence."

Unhealthy Effects of Internalizing When Cronyism Creates Harm

As a victim of cronyism, my symptoms were intensifying. I was working hard and long hours, taking on additional responsibilities; my sole focus became my job. I was neglecting all other aspects of my life-- I had no other aspect to my life. I was a workaholic. I believed my accomplishments, exemplary track record and untiring work ethic would be acknowledged and compensated; but this was not to be the case.

My spirit was being crushed; attention and accolades were bestowed upon the crony who did not earn them. I was internalizing my frustration and disappointment to the point it was affecting my health and well-being. I was also saddened as I came to the realization that no matter my efforts or achievements, my potential within the organization would never materialize.

Cronyism has often resulted in many talented and deserving people never reaching their full potential due to this detrimental practice. Imagine the great inventions, policies, etc. that have not been realized, perhaps permanently lost, to this negative "tradition".

In the late 1980's, while employed by a major technical equipment corporation, black professionals from around the country were required to participate in a week-long training course named "Corporate Efficacy."

Efficacy, as defined by Merriam-Webster, is "the power to produce a desired result or effect." Self-efficacy is the belief a person holds about whether or not he can successfully attain a desired level of performance. The self-efficacy concepts relates to motivation, performance, and emotional well-being. Corporate efficacy is when people believe their actions can produce desired outcomes in the workplace and persevere in the face of obstacles and adverse circumstances. The training was designed to better equip black professionals for psychological and emotional well-being in the corporate environment. The two key concepts were:

A. **Examine yourself for self-destructive behaviors that are impeding your success.** Learn to believe that you can – it may take one small step at a time, but each step is evidence that you are capable. Don't believe negative self-talk – other people have done this and so can I; you will really only know if you try. Use failure to learn – we have all experienced failure in some aspect. Treat failure as new information to help you improve. Understand the link between emotions and behaviors, and understand strong negative emotions can lead to self-destructive behaviors.

B. **Use the least amount of force necessary to achieve a desired outcome.** The concept is: self-control, exercise diplomacy in the workplace, minimize confrontation, work collaboratively and collectively. I fully understood the wisdom of this approach; I embraced the attitude of self-control to navigate corporate cultural waters, with more poise and enlightenment as a minority professional.

Throughout my more than 30-year career as a sales professional and entrepreneur, I have consistently done my best to adhere to these guiding tenets of controlling self-destruct behaviors and use the least amount of force necessary to achieve the desired outcome.

The Corporate Efficacy training was certainly helpful, but I don't recall the training discussing anything about cronyism. It's not likely that there is training to cope with cronyism; after all, unearned and undue leadership given as a result of cronyism covers for each other.

My cronyism experience left a particularly bad taste in my mouth. Competing on an uneven playing field with those unqualified individuals who were sponsored and unduly well-positioned, was taking a serious toll on my health and outlook.

Here is one example of the frustration I was dealing with: I was assigned a very difficult, non-producing account. My mission was to turn the account around and increase revenues. This was not an easy task! I invested a lot of time and worked to develop deep personal relationships throughout the organization. I was able to secure several long term contracts; I successfully managed to take this very challenging account and make it profitable. Before I could realize any commissionable returns, the account was turned over to a non-performing team member who was closely aligned with the "good ole boy network." And then, I was then assigned another difficult account with steadily declining returns.

I was being viewed as the "fixer upper", but was not gaining any of the remuneration! This act of cronyism was very injurious; the "connected" non-performer was reaping the financial gains of my efforts while I was earning "attaboys" for a job well done.

In the sales profession, your efforts are typically rewarded in commission compensation. All of my efforts in turning the account around were yielding financial gain for the previous non-performer, and I'm reassigned to an account with no financial benefits! I am expected to invest countless hours and efforts to make it profitable...but not for me! Cronyism left a very bitter taste in my mouth!

Overall, my life in Corporate America had many peaks and valleys. Two very significant events are forever embedded in my memory. The first one being my first position in Corporate America in a sales capacity at 26-years-old; and the second one was being fired at age 58 due to rampant cronyism.

Corporate America did afford me some very positive things, like lifelong friendships, enviable earnings, and many self-realization moments, including a better understanding of my capabilities and knowing with a plan and strategy, I can achieve what I set out to do. However, the emotional turmoil of cronyism and nepotism took its terrible toll on me.

While I endured significant misery and distress, I know now it was to fulfill a mission and calling. I would not ultimately realize this understanding until my late 50's when everything would be revealed.

My beach ball challenges and issues, age 30 to 40:

- Career Transition
- Self-pity
- Loss of Passion

What I learned from my corporate years:

- Corporate employment is a game, know the rules so you can play to win
- Morality, character, and integrity are great axioms, but not always policy or practice

- The Corporate "Aquarium" can be filled with incompatible "fish" who are predator and prey
- Check your "feelings" at the door, but never, ever compromise principle
- If you don't get what you've earned and deserve from a company, leave
- Learn to forgive those who wronged you and move on or out
- Know your value. Negotiate from a position of strength because you get what you negotiate

Exercise:
Have you had your own experience with cronyism or been treated unjustly? Take a moment to annotate the situation. If you've kept this bottled up for years, writing about it now can help to release and free you from old negativity that you may not have realized has been holding you down or preying on your conscious.

_____
_____
_____
_____
_____
_____
_____
_____
_____
_____

To fully release any emotional baggage from bad corporate situations, feel free to write what you'd like to say to the person or persons that you hold accountable

_____
_____

If you are still working for a company, do you enjoy your work? If not, why not?

Take a moment to write down five (or more) things that are a priority to you in the workplace. Do you currently have those things? If not, why not?

Deanna's Advice on How To Survive Job Turnover

At this point, you have likely spent 25+ years in the workplace. I'm certain you have your own stories of injustice or being overlooked for earned promotions and proven value for raises. All business in America - white-collar, blue-collar, professional trade, owner, etc. - has a lot of opportunity for ugliness. We are dealing with all kinds of people and personalities. A company or business or church or institution is just the "people" who run it and work in it. If you are an employee, then you are at the mercy of the employer and your direct supervisor. If you are an owner, then you depend on employees, along with quality products or services, the economy, great customer service, and a plan that you can forecast and execute, etc.

So, at any given point, we are vulnerable to others; hence, we should expect to be let down at times. I recommend you tell your story to "worthy ears", someone who cares about you, can relate to your story, and sympathize with where you have been and where you are today. Then, prepare to move on with lessons learned.

I have heard many stories of the effects of corporate downsizing. Most of the stories from people who have acquired tenure with a company typically reflect on the process prior to getting the boot as more of a long-fought battle lost. It may sound something like this: I lost a tooth-and-nail fight to maintain a position on a shrinking company roster, a company that was no longer enjoyable to work for, a company that brought more stress to my life than benefit. Those of us who jumped ship early had a head start to the next great adventure. I've often felt bad for those who were "saved" from lay-offs. Their workload increased exponentially, their resources and support decreased, and, often times, they had to endure a cut in pay while working additional long hours.

If this sounds like you, or someone you know, you can take solace knowing the stories and insight in this book can empower you to change the course of your career or job. Working at a job, or in a career that does not bring you joy, benefit, and feeling appreciated is detrimental to your health and well-being. You deserve to be happily employed!

If you are unexpectedly unemployed, then there is a (natural) grieving period when you are in transition from that job to your next venture. Take the time you need to grieve; a couple of weeks for example. If you do not take the time to acknowledge loss and change, then it will carry with you, in a negative persona until you do. It will show up in your upcoming interviews as someone who has not moved on, someone who really doesn't want to be in that chair because you still see yourself in the past and not wanting a change, or someone regretting something you did or said.

Some of you may have even loved what you did and who you worked for. If this is the case, it is just as important for you to take the time you need to process that your good job, working for a good company, has ended. You are probably wondering if it will ever be that good again. Are you going to have to "settle" for less pay and fewer benefits since you are re-entering the workforce at a later age? No!

Research has been documented that up to 70 percent of white-collar workers are unhappily employed, yet still working over 60 hours per week. If you find yourself in this category, I challenge you to re-imagine yourself and what career or company you wish to pursue. You are not too old, or under-educated, or irrelevant! I'm also speaking to those who find themselves underemployed.

You can move on and up after a change in your employment status, and you can be doing something you love to do! Not often, but every once in awhile, I have a client who just cannot imagine this fact, no matter how hard we try to "re-vision" them. They just cannot see themselves making the necessary moves to do what they really want to do. They actually *believe* it is not possible for them. For those clients, I share this story:

Many years ago, in an Indian village, a farmer had the misfortune of owing a large sum of money to the village moneylender. The old and ugly moneylender fancied the farmer's beautiful, young daughter, so he proposed a bargain. He would forgive the farmer's debt if he could marry his daughter. Both the farmer and his daughter were horrified by the proposal, but the cunning moneylender suggested they let providence decide the matter. He told them he would put a black pebble and a white pebble into an empty money bag.

The girl would have to reach in and pick one pebble from the bag. If she picked the black pebble, she would become his wife and her father's debt would be forgiven. If she picked the white pebble, she need not marry him and her father's debt would still be forgiven. If she refused to pick a pebble, her father would be thrown into jail until the debt was paid.

They were standing on a pebble-strewn path in the farmer's field. As they talked, the moneylender bent over to pick up two pebbles. The sharp-eyed girl noticed he picked up two black pebbles and put them into the bag. He then asked the girl to pick a pebble. Now, imagine you were the girl standing in the field. What would you have done? If you had to advise her, what would you have told her?

Careful analysis would produce three possibilities: (1) The girl could refuse to take a pebble, but her father would be thrown in jail. (2) The girl could pick a black pebble and sacrifice herself in order to save her father from debt and imprisonment. Or, (3) the girl could pull out both black pebbles in the bag, expose the moneylender as a cheat, and likely incite his immediate revenge.

Take a moment to think through this story. I've used it with the hope it will help you see alternate solutions beyond the obvious ones. The girl's dilemma cannot be solved with traditional logical thinking. You may be in a similar situation. You may be in a job you hate, but the pay is great. You have two choices: (1) You can stay in a job you hate. (2) You can leave the job, but you will then give up the great pay. Are these really all of the options?

Okay, back to our girl with the two pebbles in the bag. Here is what the girl did:

She put her hand into the money bag and drew out a pebble. Without looking at it, she fumbled and let it fall onto the pebble-strewn path, where it immediately became lost among all the other pebbles. "Oh, how clumsy of me," she said, "but never mind, if you look into the bag for the one that is left, you will be able to tell which pebble I picked." Since the remaining pebble was black, it would have to be assumed she had picked the white one. And, since the moneylender dared not admit his dishonesty, the girl would have changed what seemed an impossible situation into an extremely advantageous one.

Again, when God has placed a dream in your heart, He has already provisioned the path...so, let's figure it out together. But, first, *you* have to *believe* it is possible!

Job Search Strategy

One thing that is a continuous challenge for me when coaching us "Over 50's" in beginning a new career or job search is the fact today's approach in gaining meaningful and fulfilling employment is polar opposite from how we've ever approached it before. In addition, we will tend to seek after a position or career path that mirrors our past experiences or credentials - but not our real, authentic, truest passion.

Now, I understand if you are currently unemployed, versus underemployed or unhappily employed, finding employment quickly will lean heavily on framing your past experiences and credentials; however, I want to focus on finding work you truly love.

Since I started over, in 2008, I have been a faithful follower of Dan Miller, author and entrepreneur. His book, "48 Days to the Work You Love", has been the foundation layer of my coaching. I attended Dan's workshop in 2009 to become a certified coach in delivering his "48 Days to the Work You Love" seminar. I love having a front row seat in witnessing the complete transformation of those who commit to finding their true, God-ordained talent and gifts, and watch as they follow the steps to fulfilling their purpose. I add an additional layer to Dan's proven method, and that is the view from the "hiring side" of the desk with over 20 years' experience putting together award-winning sales teams.

Our generation averages *five* jobs in a lifetime. Today's Millennials will have from *19-25 jobs, averaging 13-18 months* per employer. We were always taught the longer you stay at a job was better representation on your résumé - it showed loyalty. That is no longer the case, and frankly hasn't been for quite a while. Employers want to see risk-takers, embracers of new technology, and creative talent lacking nothing in the passion and enthusiasm department.

At this point, I would ask a client this: Would you hire you? Hoping that, without hesitation, they would say, confidently, YES! Now, *why* would you hire you? That would be the beginning of charting out your value statement. Unfortunately, some of us are thinking of why a prospective employer would NOT hire us, like, "I don't have a college education." Or, "I am Over 50." Or, "The trade I've been doing for almost 30 years is no longer needed."...

I promise you, there is great value you can offer to a company, or offer as a service for self-employment. It is in you and has been in you for many years.

Let's first talk about "de-aging" your résumé. Although it is against the law to discriminate against our protected age group, it is unfortunately still practiced. So, what we will create instead, is an advertisement for an interview that does not give away our age, but still frames our experience. Keep in mind, the résumé's *only* purpose is to advertise for an interview. Once we gain the interview, we will win them over with our value, confidence, and relevance.

Here are some ways your résumé may make you look over 50:

1.) Including a middle initial or your middle name

2.) Displaying your full address. This is not recommended simply for your personal safety, but also for the potential of economic profiling

3.) Including more numbers than your mobile number. If you are uncomfortable placing your personal cell number, then obtain a Google Voice number as your mobile number. It can be set-up so that it will ring on multiple phones and can be configured to transcribe the message, which can then be emailed and/or texted to you

4.) Using an email address that is either aol.com or has reference to a cable company. Obtain a Gmail email address or a forwarded email address from an alumni association or a professional society or association. Ideally, it would be great if you secured your name as your URL (i.e. maxgilreath.com), then use your personal domain for email

5.) Including the year you graduated college. Let's just leave that off. In some cases, it may be before the hiring manager was born. If you are, however, a recent graduate, then certainly include the date

6.) Double-spacing after a period. I'll be honest, this was a hard habit to break for me. It is a sure give-away we are "older" when displayed throughout your résumé. Double-spacing after a period is not even taught anymore

7.) Including an objective statement, which the majority of the time is all about *you* and what *you* want, the company (at this point) doesn't care. It reminds me of a quote from Chick-fil-A founder Truett Cathy, he said; "We don't hire *you* because *you* need a job, we hire you because *we* need you. So, no objective statement...period

8.) If you can help it, try not to go back more than 10-15 years of professional experience. Most certainly, do not list the jobs you held back in the 80's or 90's. If you find that your past experiences, or significant achievements, bring great value to the targeted position you are applying for, then I would recommend you summarize "additional experience" and leave off the pertinent dates associated with those experiences. One exception would be if you served in the military. Frame your service on your résumé, not the tenure. (i.e. served in the U.S Army for 4 years (not from 1980-1984)). If you served in the military, I want to personally honor, and sincerely thank you for your bravery and for the unselfish sacrifice you and your family extended to all of us! Now, back to de-aging...

9.) Don't list "run-of-the-mill" skills like MS Word, PowerPoint, or Excel. It makes it look as if you've just gotten onboard with those programs

10.) You absolutely do not want to list a fax number, pager number, or how many words per minute you type

Since your résumé will get about a 10-20 second initial look by someone before they decide to read further and place you in the "call 'em" pile, you at least do not want to be quickly eliminated due to "old school" ways.

For strategy, we are taking a play out of the hockey great, Wayne Gretzky's, playbook: Someone once asked Mr. Gretzky "What makes you such a great hockey player?" Wayne answered, "A good hockey player plays where the puck is. A great hockey player plays where the puck is going to be." Now, paraphrasing that for our purposes, "That's easy - I go to where the puck is going to be, everyone else goes to where it is." That is how we approach job search: Where the jobs are going to be.

Do not confuse this with the old "boomer" way of plotting a career. We were likely taught you pick a college major or career path based on the projections of highest volume of job availability for a certain position (or what you're good at, not necessarily what you like or love to do). Going to where the jobs are going to be is based on the fact you have already uncovered your desired vocation, one that aligns directly with your passion, skills, abilities, and dreams.

Here are some statistics that may help narrow your search opportunity and save you some time. I am grateful to Dan Miller, author of "48 Days to the Work You Love" for most of these points:

Over 50% of new positions available are in companies with less than 100 employees.

Only 3% of the available jobs are at "Fortune 100" companies. We can increase your success rate for job offers if we focus on more of the smaller companies (employee-wise) rather than the larger ones.

Public job posts represent less than 20% of the jobs available. We will be outlining how to go about marketing to the 80%+ jobs that are *not* public knowledge and *those* results are at an impressive **86% success rate.**

First, here are some facts to compare this 86% with (These are from Dan Miller's "48 Days to the Work You Love" workbook.):

Mass response to Internet ads. The ads at Indeed.com, CareerBuilder.com, or Dice.com look so perfect to you. Just keep in mind whatever you see, thousands of other great candidates see as well. While there are exceptions to everything, the results here are pretty dismal. **Fewer than 1%** of job seekers actually get a position from responding to an Internet ad.

Here is my analogy on this: **C.R.A.P.** - **C**lick, **R**eview, **A**pply, **P**ray. Another great reason not to post your résumé to these sites is the endless amounts of spam you will receive through text and email. Also, you cannot turn it off. Once you get your dream job, your résumé is still out there giving the appearance that you are still seeking a job.

Answering ads in trade journals leads to jobs for **7 out of 100**. (Too much time delay for proactive searching, etc.)

Answering local ads, i.e. Facebook or Craigslist, leads to jobs for about **8 out of 100**. (NOTE: The higher the level the job you seek, the less effective this method is.)

Recruiter and headhunter pursuit lead to jobs for **4 - 22 out of 100**. (Again, depending on the level sought.) No one can present you as well as you can or cares about your situation as much as you do. Headhunters and executive recruiters get paid by the companies that hire them to fill their open positions, so where exactly is their loyalty? With their client companies. Recruiters will not market job-seekers to companies; instead, they try to fit job-seekers into well-defined positions with the companies that employ their services. Some larger companies for executive positions will require this route. In those cases, it is always nice when the hiring manager decides to hire you, and *then* sends you through the recruiter for "processing".

Using the placement office at the school or college you once attended leads to a job for **21 out of 100.**

Asking relatives for job leads gets a job for about **27 out of 100.**

Asking friends for job leads gets a job for **34 out of 100.** (Don't be hesitant about letting others know what you are looking for.)

Applying directly to an employer without doing any homework leads to a job for **47 out of 100**. (Just walking in the door, unannounced, works almost half the time. Notice, this is the second most effective method, but it works best for lower-level positions. Dan Miller's proactive approach is the first at an **86%** success rate.)

Are these people happy with their new employers? Do they stay? Are you ready to deploy the plan that works better than any of these *and* lands you a job you love faster?

Have you ever heard finding a job is a full-time job? I recommend dedicating at least 35 hours per week to your job search. Yes, you read that right: Dedicate at least 35 hours per week to include networking, researching companies, making contact, follow-up, volunteering, and interview preparedness. And yes, this process is intense, but when you are laser focused, it is the quickest strategy that yields top quality job offers.

First, make a list of the top 15-25 companies you would like to target for employment and why they would be a good candidate for the value you bring. Be creative and diversify your list to include companies of all sizes while also keeping in mind the ones with less than 100 employees represent 50% of the hiring opportunities.

Here are some ideas as to how to start your list:

- They could be geographically chosen, something close to where you live, or close to where a friend/colleague works who you would like to carpool with
- Perhaps, they are a great cultural fit for you, as in a faith-based company, for instance
- I encourage clients to look into companies where they love the product or service because when you are genuinely passionate about their product or service, it translates to enthusiasm and likability on an interview
- Perhaps, the company is on the "best place to work" list for your city - those make great candidates to target for employment, and you have an easy subject to begin dialog over
- Do you want a start-up or a more established employer?
- Ask people you know who are happy with their company where they work and place those companies on your list
- You can also approach creating your list from a vertical perspective: Healthcare, Non-Profit, Manufacturing, Education, Technology, Apparel, etc.

Do your research on these companies. A great way to research, other than Google and Yelp, etc., is Hoovers.com.

The smaller, private companies will need a little more effort to research; however, in the long run, you want to be well educated and informed on any potential employer. Be empowered to choose the companies you would like to work with.

You don't have to wait until a company advertises a position, or you hear someone say a company is hiring. Those usual methods typically put you up against 70 to 80 people for almost any desirable position; whereas, in this method, you may have only 2 to 3 true competitors.

You must recognize that when you see an ad for a particular position, you may have already lost your best opportunity for that position. Also, this is the method for finding the 80+ percent of the jobs that are never advertised. In a rapidly changing workplace, everyone is looking for good people.

Be proactive in your search - go where the jobs are going to be before they advertise the need for a new position.

Next, you will draft an introduction letter for the top companies on your target list. I recommend you send out no more than 10 per day, as the most important part of the process is follow-up, follow-up, follow-up.

The introduction letter is to build your name and brand recognition. Remember, you are the product, and you are the marketer and sales representative for your product. In advertising and sales, it is about "customer touches". That is what we are doing with the introduction letter. It is our initial company touch.

With this introduction letter that represents your "brand", I like to use unique fonts for your stationary (your name at the top of the letter). It will match your résumé, and, therefore, become a recognizable marketing piece.

For those who are seeking high-end positions, especially in marketing or sales, I recommend creating a personal logo. Something that will differentiate you from other job seekers. Research who to address the cover letter to - you are going for a *personal* connection.

The company website or LinkedIn.com, is a great resource to find who the hiring manager would be, so no "To Whom It May Concern" or "Attention Hiring Manager". In today's technology, it is too easy to find the name and title of the best person to address for your letter. With LinkedIn, you can do searches by company and it will show you who you know there, or who you are connected with who is connected to someone from that company. All the more reason to build up your LinkedIn connections...as if you needed another incentive.

The content of your introduction letter should include a reason for the introduction (*not* seeking a job yet, but making an introduction to connect and begin to build a relationship with the company). Any recent news-worthy event you can mention is the best way to break the ice.

The introduction letter has *no* call-to-action - it's only purpose is to introduce yourself and make an initial connection. I recommend sending out in "snail mail" with a follow-up copy in email form about four days later. If you time it right, the hiring manager will get the "snail mail" and email copy the same day, resulting in your first two touches.

Finally, you will draft cover letters to accompany your résumé and send them out a week after your introduction letters. A professional, printed copy of your resume in a real envelope is still the most respected method of first contact.

The content of the cover letter needs to be positioned as to the value you will bring to an organization. It should reflect the company's currency and grab their attention immediately. For example, if you are pursuing a customer service position, the "currency for value" may be "increased customer satisfaction by 10%" or "achieved 99% favorability on customer survey" or "decreased churn by 12%"...

Remember, it isn't about *you* needing a job; it is about the *company's need* for the most valuable candidate.

Tailor each cover letter for each targeted company, although the body of the letter could remain the same, modify the reason why you are targeting that particular company. Tell a story, do not just list your skills.

At the end of your letter, the "call to action" is to ask for fifteen minutes to come by and meet them in person.

Lastly, state a day and time of when you will be calling them to follow-up. *Never* end a letter to a prospective employer as "looking forward to hearing from you". Always place the follow-up in this process on you, proactively.

You are making an initial connection and starting a relationship. People hire people who are confident, enthusiastic and likeable. Once you make these connections, it is not a matter of *if* they hire you, but *when*. Sometimes, your targeted hiring manager doesn't have an open position but will sponsor you to a colleague who does.

Please allow me to tell you *why* this is so effective in my opinion and works from the view of a hiring manager: Hiring managers, and the average hiring process in today's workforce, are not what they used to be.

Medium to small companies (the hiring sweet spot in America) often do not have the luxury of recruiters or human resource departments to fill their candidate funnel to ensure they have a team of productive, innovative, energized staff to carry out their business plan and goals. In fact, most times, a manager is holding onto current employees who are underperforming (and thus likely unhappily employed) simply because they do not have time to pursue quality candidates.

They would rather keep a team member who is half-productive and negative than face the task of placing an ad and having to go through hundreds of applicants, setting up interviews, doing background checks, checking and chasing down references, and then hiring, training and bringing a new person up to speed.

How sad is that? *This* is *why* this process works so well. Being in sales management for many years, had I been approached by a professional in this matter, I could actually see moving under-performers off the team to make way for someone who actually wants to work for my team (and be grateful they took the time to eliminate some of my stress).

One of my favorite bosses was a former Marine who once told me, "Poehlman, shoot the trailing dog and the pack will speed up". Nothing makes a team increase their stride or improve productivity more than seeing their manager interviewing candidates.

This process actually allows you to take a cut in the line, to be the top of the résumé pile for potential employment. It may eliminate their need to advertise for a position *and* save the company a lot of lost productivity and cost associated in candidate recruitment.

Now, for the most important part of the process: Follow-up! If you have no intention of personally following up with a phone call, then do not bother to send out letters and résumés. My experience is only about 3 percent of job hunters do this, **only 3%**!

Dan Miller notes if you just send letters and résumés *without* following up with a call, then you will need to send out **254** to have a statistical chance of getting a job offer. *But*, if you combine your efforts with the follow-up call, then that number drops to 1 out of 15 - what a dramatic difference a little extra effort makes! This is a selling process. We use these multiple customer touches in the process because that is the basis of understanding marketing principles.

To enhance your success for job offers in this process, engage in networking activities. Not for social reasons, but for the specific purpose of getting face-to-face with professionals in your community and communicate the value you would bring to their organization and specifically why.

Have your elevator speech ready *at all times* when you are in all places: The grocery store, getting your oil changed, social events, church, etc. Be prepared to confidently articulate how they can help you in this process, like what would be a good company match and what value you exclusively bring. Have some business cards printed with your value statement, what you are looking for, and your contact information.

In summary, the five critical steps of job search strategy are:

1. Make a list of 15-25 companies you want to target to work for and *why*
2. Send introduction letter to each
3. Send cover letter and résumé a week later and ask for meeting
4. Follow-up, follow-up, follow-up
5. Network, get out from behind that computer screen, and no more CRAP - Click, Review, Apply, Pray. Well, I do recommend the pray part, but after the above process is followed

See the **20-Day Plan for Job Transition** at over50startingover.net for a detailed process. In addition, there is a resource tab that directs you to free technology training and many other valuable resources.

CHAPTER SIX

Gain, Loss, Gain
WTH Happened

The 1980's

My second son, "Jay", was born in 1981, less than two years before I began my new career in the computer and technical equipment sector. Throughout my adult life, I unfortunately did not maintain a balance between career and family life. Like so many families in America, my wife and I had new careers, hers in healthcare procurement and mine in Information Technology (IT) equipment sales, one son, age seven, and the other, an infant.

We were a close-knit and very loving family. As parents, both my wife and I were hands-on and deeply involved in their education and overall growth and development. We both worked hard to guide and mold our children, in ways we were not afforded in our youth. We made sure our children had the best education opportunities and were exposed to a multiple of extracurricular activities. Our sons were both intellectually capable, motivated, and athletically inclined.

As a father, I showered my sons with affection and told them daily I loved them. I made sure I reversed those imprints in my youth, and, more than a generation later, we still share the joy of a hearty hug and kiss. I think for most parents few things are more heart-felt than to see your child or children walk into a room, no matter their age. My sons are now 42 and 35, but I will always see them as the small, innocent boys they once were. Such beautiful and good boys who are now beautiful and good men.

Thinking back over the past 40-plus years, I can say, without reservation, I gave my children as much love as I possibly could, even while coping with my own internal demons, specifically anger-related issues. I'm blessed and honored to have fathered two loving, caring, sincere, authentic, respectful, and smart men. They are the two most significant accomplishments of my life, and I thank God for them. The 80's was a decade of discovery in all life's aspects: family, career, spiritual development, and physical maturity. Still in my 20's, I had a sense of accomplishment with both my family and career.

The 80's were also a time for new friendships of my Houston, Texas-based and extended "Life Team" - Scott, Robert, Rudy, Gene, Chuck, Dennis and Donald. All, with exception of Robert who is now deceased, have been friends of mine for more than thirty years (More about the "Life Team" concept in subsequent chapters). All of our families were very close - we camped out together, worked together, raised our families together...and started over after divorce together. I've always been blessed to have great people in my life - "Be a friend to have a friend." I have lived my life by this motto and credo.

The 1990's

Now, in my 30's, with a stable career and great family, I had a (mistaken) sense of invincibility in every aspect of my life. I think most people have a time or period in life when everything seems (almost too) perfect. I call it the "sweet spot", where if I could make time stand still, I would. For me, it was between 1988 and 1990, from ages thirty-two to thirty-four. I had been married for more than fifteen years, with two growing boys and no family deaths. Unknowingly, I had entered the 1990's - the decade which would become that of heart-breaking losses and life-changing circumstances.

In 1991, I attended a Jazz Fest in Cancun, and met a great group of guys there from Los Angeles and Atlanta, developing a rapport that has endured to this day. They helped me realize my dream of moving to California, regaining my zest for life, providing my family an opportunity to experience a more eclectic life amidst a backdrop of sandy beaches and rolling blue-green waters of the Pacific Ocean - a life I often dreamed of as a young man. My Los Angeles and Atlanta "Life Team" of Charles, Verdell, Daryl, Gary, and Ken would continue to grow in depth and friendship over the years.

That same year, I learned I had a heart condition and became depressed. As the first Black Sales Manager over my work environment, which was toxic, suppressive, and prejudiced, I was under a physician's care for more than a year. A generation ago, depression was considered by many to be an unfounded illness, especially in the black community.

When I got the diagnosis, I had a sense of shame in that I knew I would be perceived as weak. Therefore, other than my wife and a few close friends, I kept it to myself. Even my wife, though supportive, did not know the breadth and depth of the emotional turmoil I was experiencing. The heart condition was non-life-threatening; however, I had to take medications and maintain proper blood pressure levels. So, I have taken various blood pressure meds for more than thirty years.

After being out of work for several months due to depression and the heart condition, I agreed to accept (after 10 years of service) a severance package from my employer, and focus on my son's, "Jody," high school graduation and his transition to college, where he had earned a track-and-field scholarship. I was so proud my son had talents, which mirrored my own, and, with the guidance and support of my wife and me, he had the grades and the athleticism to earn a full scholarship.

We "boomers" gave up so much as we were growing up – be it from parents who didn't encourage us, or finances that weren't there, or whatever the case may be – that we typically take particular pride when our children accomplish great things, especially when those things parallel, or mirror, that which we had aspired to, but circumstances prevented.

Over the past ten to fifteen years, depression has become recognized as a legitimate and serious medical condition, whether as biological disorder or event induced. Even today, people think depression is nothing more than "having a bad day" weakness. But, I can tell you from very personal experience that "having a bad day" is *not* weakness when one is caught in the downward spiral of depression - one's whole outlook and worldview may be profoundly negative, with a loss of hope, debilitating fatigue, and, for many, even suicide. It is imperative to seek professional help and counsel if you (or anyone you know) have any of these symptoms. For me, my physician was the only person who I could truly open up to and share my deepest, darkest feelings. There were three things that helped me cope and got me through the darkness of depression:

1. Professional diagnosis and counsel
2. Strict diet and exercise for my Mind-Body-Spirit
3. My family

Empty Nest, Relational Loss, Divorce and Financial Shift:

In the early 90's, my mother was diagnosed with dementia and Alzheimer's. Her memory was in and out and rapidly diminishing. When I would visit from Texas, there were times when she would remember the names of her children and everyone around her, and then, there were times when she would look at me with her warm smile and not know who I was. This absolutely broke my heart to see my mother in that condition.

Many of my siblings and I learned to deal with her illness with humor - this was the single best coping mechanism I had, coupled with my memories of her before the ravages of Alzheimer's. It really is "the disease of the long goodbye."

My father, Dwight, was deeply affected by my mother's condition. He was devastated by her loss of memory and inability to communicate with him as they had done so for so many years. I believe he felt helpless and hopeless as he no longer knew how to cope with her condition. Though I lived in California at the time, I had a sense of what was going on with my parents, both through communicating with siblings and knowing the dynamics of my parents' relationship.

Father's gym was in the basement of our family homestead, filled with fitness equipment that he had designed and engineered himself from the 1950's into the 1980's. His gym was where he would go not just for exercise and fitness, but also for refuge and escape, as well as for mental and psychological comfort.

One day, my brother called and told me our father had fallen and hit his head on an iron weight in his gym. He had to be hospitalized due to the impact to his brain. Ultimately, he would succumb to this head injury, due to brain aneurysm at age 83. The year was 1993 - the same year my son "Jody" would graduate from high school. Not since Uncle Ken had passed more than twenty-five years earlier, had someone so close to me as my father passed away.

The same year my father passed, my wife and I agreed when Jody graduated from high school and went off to college, we would pick up and move to Los Angeles. But, when the time came to move, things changed. My wife decided she wanted to stay in Texas, and I would move to Los Angeles get settled, and, then, she and our son would move there. This would be the 'foyer' to empty nesters, as well as the foundation leading to vulnerability and, in my case, ultimately divorce.

Jody was 18, entering college, while Jay was 12 years old. Our nest was half empty. The warning signs of impending conflict between my wife and I were clearly a problem, however due to the absence of communication, we ignored them.

I was determined to leave Texas and make California our new home, and so I did. Jenny was concerned about uprooting from Houston for such a quantum leap to Los Angeles. Between my wife and I, we maintained two households for more than two years. Long-distance relationships can take a toll on not just a husband and wife, but the rest of family, and ours was no exception.

Even though I was not very emotionally close to my father, I still loved him and tried to focus only on the positives from his legacy. While he has some negative traits, as we all do, he was a good man with many good and positive traits. When a parent passes away, it has a way of magnifying a child's focus on mortality. Up to the point of my father's passing, only my mother was sick. However, to our surprise, it was my father who was the first parent to pass away in 1993. I had a somewhat false sense of immortality, fostered by youth and the denial that one day I too will die.

Two years later, in 1995, my mother passed away at age 81. The death of my beloved mother ripped my heart out. She was my first love, and any woman that I would marry would need to have similar standards and qualities. She was an amazing woman! She embraced my wife as her own daughter. Of all the girls I brought home to meet my mother, Jenny was the one whom my mother truly embraced and loved.

I was just coming to terms with my father's passing two years earlier, and now, I was dealing with the intense grief of my mother, now gone as well. My parents were married for more than 50 years. Numerous studies have indicated it is quite common for spouses to pass relatively close to one another when they have been together for 50 years or more. At the time, I was not aware of this phenomenon. I was grief stricken - both of my parents were gone! They were the nucleus that kept our extended family together. By visiting at their home in North Carolina, we would all gather as a family. I dealt with their loss, in part, through remembering the good times and feeling blessed that both my sons had the opportunity to know their grandparents.

Parental loss and the connected emotions are as intense as personal love lost. The five stages of mourning and grief are experienced in different ways by every individual. Bereavement can be difficult, with the healing process in no specific sequence (and sometimes, it's two steps forward, one step back):

1. Denial and Isolation
2. Anger and regret (as in if only I had said/done…?)
3. Bargaining
4. Depression
5. Acceptance

Everyone experiences the bereavement process in a different way. For me, denial, isolation, and depression were my significant challenges leading to acceptance. It took me far longer to find acceptance with my mother's passing than my father's, primarily because I was closer to my mother than my father. Deaths of my father and mother and feeling a general lack of control over my own life led to a profound sensation of emptiness, a lack of meaning, and a loss of self.

There are no shortcuts in the healing process. Please read that statement again. It took years for me to finally let go, accept, and move on. There were many times when I could not celebrate Mother's Day, or even acknowledge it without my mother. Not even bothering to go outside, I would stay in bed all day. Yet, I always acknowledged both of my mother and father's birthdays, their anniversary, Valentine's Day, and Christmas.

Though they have been gone for more than 20 years now, I still think of them, especially during these special days and holidays we shared. In hindsight, I probably could have coped with their losses much better had I sought out professional counsel. When experiencing depression or bereavement, it is so important to have a third party professional who one can open up to without judgment or ridicule.

Now living in Los Angeles, I quickly adapted to the Californian culture and versatility for adding another dimension to my life. I embraced it as an opportunity to start fresh, with a new perspective, passion, and goal for both me and my family. I adjusted well to life in California and had developed a network of good friends - I was filled with passion and new energies for life and the future. However, I still felt a sense of emptiness and longing for my family and parents.

In 1994, I started, and personally funded (in part because I saw this as a new career), a non-profit foundation in Los Angeles named "Maximize Leadership Foundation", focused on minority children in the first through fourth grades, helping them to develop leadership skills and elevate their self-esteem. My motivation was based upon the need to give something back to the community that I had quickly embraced. The community welcomed me and the value of the curriculum and programs. This compelled me to make an impact and give of my time and resources. I aligned the foundation with a well-known African-American church in Los Angeles.

I worked with the children, mentoring them in leadership and self-esteem skills for a few years. This was one of the most gratifying things I had ever done, and it helped me cope with missing my own family. Sadly, due to lack of additional financial funding, I had to close the foundation in 1995.

Then, I went back to work as a sales professional for another major corporation in the telecommunications sector. We had set aside enough money to move my wife and son to Los Angeles. Although I visited them in Houston on a regular basis, we had been living apart for more than two years.

When they arrived in 1996, I was so excited to have them with me again as a family. But, things had changed - my wife and I had grown in different directions. My son immediately embraced California culture; however, my wife was uncomfortable with and unsure of the move.

We found ourselves uncommunicative and unresponsive to each other, as if we were strangers. This can happen when two people stop communicating and cease being honest with each other about their deepest-felt feelings. I learned there's no greater time of vulnerability in a married relationship than with empty (or partial) nest or long distance apart – it can set the stage for relationship ruin.

My youngest son, "Jay", was now in high school, my career was going well, and I was working on a major project on the coast of California while my wife was looking for work. Of course, like any couple, we had our ups and downs, arguments, and periods of anxiety. But, this time, it was more like two strangers trying to get to know each other. It felt weird and strange.

My wife, a woman I had known since we were seven years old, the woman I had been married to for over 20 years, had changed. Actually, we both had changed. We weren't able to communicate, to talk to each other and it seemed as if we had each built walls around ourselves. We lived together, but now slept in separate bedrooms. We were not connecting on any level. My son was aware of the distance between us, and his behavior changed. He started acting out emotionally and hanging out with the wrong crowd of kids.

The dysfunctional relationship between my wife and me went on for a while. Then, one day, I came home, and she handed me the divorce decree. Simple as that. I have to say, I was surprised but not shocked. I knew something had to give - I just did not know the form in which it would take. We discussed it briefly with little emotion, and then, I went for a drive, totally "fogged out", just numb! When I returned, we briefly discussed the details for proceeding forward with the divorce. Afterward, I simply went to bed.

As Jenny and I went through the process of divorce, we agreed she would move back to Houston, and "Jay" would stay with me. Then, we matter-of-factly divided up our property and other material possessions and set milestone dates. One evening, I came home from work, and the movers had picked up the things she wanted (as we had agreed), and, just like that, she was moved out, heading back to her life in Houston.

My son was at a friend's house, and I sat in an empty living room with a beer. I was lost, in unchartered territory! When everything goes awry and there's no quick fix or solution, you're in THE PIT, not knowing how to get out of this deep abyss.

"Starting Over", now as a single man in my forties, I put my focus on my son and getting him on stable ground. But, he grew even angrier, acting out in school more, and I found myself visiting his teachers and principal several times a week, all while working sixty-plus hours, including weekends.

"Jay" would stay with neighbors or friends when I was traveling. Talk about stress! Eventually, "Jay" was expelled from school. I searched desperately for a public, private, or military school that would meet his needs, but, unfortunately, to no avail. At only 16, he moved back to Texas, and began living with his friends, somewhere close to San Marcos, TX, where his brother was in college near there. He did this on his own, without parental guidance or directive.

I was in a tailspin - depressed, drinking a lot, working seven days a week, dealing with being a divorcee, and my son moving out. Then, one evening, I got a conference call from my friends in both Houston and California, partly in show of support and friendship, but also to make sure I was okay. All I could think about was my sons and how stupid mistakes had led to divorce, all because we could not communicate our true feelings, wants, and needs.

I hung up the phone and wept for what seemed like hours. That Sunday, I went to church with my friend, Charles, and his wife. During the service, I broke down and wailed like I've never cried before. It came from someplace so deep within me that my cheeks and lungs ached. I had never felt such a sense of loss, grief, failure, and utter sadness in my life. I was doubled over in a seated fetal position, crying, while people from all over the congregation gathered around me in prayer, love, and support.

I had hit ROCK BOTTOM, which is so low that there's no other direction but up. I had previously dealt with deep depression that kept me out of work, the deaths of both parents, leaving my family in Houston - these are all very traumatic. Rock bottom was a culmination of all of these, along with divorce, my son moving out, and burnout from work. I had two choices: 1.) Rebuild from the bottom up, or 2.) Die. That night, I prayed to God: Either take me in my sleep, or give me the strength to repair my life and find a way to go on. When I awoke the next morning, I thanked God for the second chance, got up, and began to slowly move forward.

Weak and vulnerable, I just took it one day at a time until the divorce was final, in 1997. After the "fog" cleared, my deep sorrow shifted from myself to my sons and the deep guilt I felt for what the divorce did to them. I forgave my wife, but it would be years before I could (and would) forgive myself. Taught about the power of forgiveness since my early years of attending Sunday School, now as a grown man, I discovered how real and truly powerful it is in practice, especially when used for one's own self.

"I believe that a couple's relationship can never be more vulnerable than when the nest is empty" - Max Gilreath

Growing up, I had heard there are tribes in the Native American culture who believe manhood does not begin until age 40. Based upon my life's journey, I would characterize this as being correct, at least as experienced in my own life. At 40, men may grow to a place of foundational security in their mature being, based upon responsibility, being an adult male, leaving youth and childhood behind, living and exhibiting such qualities as strength and courage.

Within a five-year period, I experienced four major transitional challenges: empty nest, relational loss, divorce, and financial shift. I learned guilt and regret are tools of darkness, designed to prevent light from entering. While darkness harbors fear, sorrow, and the unknown, it is light that creates hope and new beginnings. Throughout my adult life, it has been the ability to forgive others (and now myself) that opened God's grace into my life.

I also learned the power of intent and how *un*intentional mistakes are far easier to forgive than the intentional ones. It is the separation of the behavior from the person that matters most. I never meant to hurt anyone, especially my family - my mistakes were unintentional; however, there are also unintended consequences for our mistakes and choices. None of us are perfect. We are all human.

Forty, divorced, and alone now (with both sons back in Texas), everything that mattered to me was gone. As a man, I was diminished. As a husband and father, I was a failure. It's true - for many men, divorce is viewed as *failure*, while for many women, it seems to be viewed as a *mistake*.

Men internalize and women verbalize, before they can speak of their loss; Written in: *Open to Hope, Finding Hope After Loss*. This is referring to the death of a spouse or loved one. However I refer to divorce as "the death of a relationship", for men it can create harbor more deeply pain and scars of such loss, because we know society may think we're weak if we share or discuss how the pain affects us. We are taught this by our parents and family, our peers, media, and society as a whole from a young age. All of my adult life, I've seen the ravages of holding everything in and onto the guilt and failure of divorce for men. And, I've experienced it first-hand. Guilt has a way of stripping a man of his spirit, passion, and fulfillment, like an invisible cancer that embeds itself in a man's heart and soul.

I felt I had no one to really talk to, even my closest friends - even when my parents were alive, emotional matters were never discussed between us. There are times in life when situations and/or circumstances are so personal and private, they are only between you and God!

My personal life was at its lowest ebb; however, my career was thriving. Talk about a paradox. I won a major telecomm project. With an emotionally empty tank, I moved forward, and planned a vacation to Puerto Vallarta, Mexico to get away from everything (and everyone) for soul-searching and healing.

I took my Bible and a copy of the book "Celestine Prophecy" with me and let every word engulf my spirit and imagination. The message of finding and sensing the energy in God's every creation helped to re-center my anxious mind and restless thoughts. It also got me back on track for fitness and working out. I needed to detox from alcohol and cigars in a big, fresh way. Newly divorced and toxic in Mind-Body-Spirit, I needed time to heal.

I became very introspection about life and my mistakes, and how they all could have been resolved or prevented, had I possessed the courage, tools, and wisdom for guidance. Alone, with an empty nest, guilt and shame were woven into a heavy quilt of torment. My waking thoughts and sleep-filled nightmares, were focused on what I had lost versus what I still had in my life. I had stopped being thankful for all of the blessings that remained, including a bright future ahead.

What if I had communicated my most intimate thoughts and feelings to my wife? What if I had not been so selfish? What if I had been more mature and discerning? What if's only created more what if's. I never experienced seeing or hearing my parents, open up to each other, even when my siblings and I knew there were problems between them. Since I didn't have an example to guide me, I had no roadmap to follow. Like so much of my early life, I had to learn by trial and error. Now, I needed to focus on lessons learned and resolutions, for "Starting Over" with a new life. Leave nothing unsaid and undone.

Once in Puerto Vallarta, I was at the hotel pool, reading. There, I noticed three women swimming. They were American. I had been reading for quite a while and decided to take a break and engage in conversation.

It seemed an eternity since I had relaxed enough to converse with total strangers. I introduced myself and learned they were from Phoenix, AZ. The lady who took the lead in the conversation was named Tiffany, and she was 27 years old, single with a young son.

Tiffany's spirit was joyful, genuine, and she was just so kind and sweet. I went to dinner that evening with her and her friends, and we all had a great time. She had what we would call in the South as "an old soul", much more mature than her years. Later, I would learn from her friends she was referred to as an "angel", and, as I got to know her better (once we returned to the States), we became very close friends.

She came to California several times to visit me, and we spoke several times weekly via phone. She made me feel alive again. One time, while visiting me, she stood up and lost her balance for no apparent reason. I asked if she had injured her ankle or foot. While she did express her concern over loss of circulation in her foot, she was very nonchalant about it. Tiffany was a swimmer (a very good one - she swam in college competitively), and she was still in top physical condition. She shared with me she had her appendix removed only a few months earlier and came to Puerto Vallarta for some post-surgery healing and relaxation.

We developed a great friendship, and I planned to visit her in Phoenix. As I said, we talked with each other several times a week; however, this week, when I didn't receive a return call from her, I chalked it up to her being busy with work and her young son. But still, I didn't hear from her all week, which was unusual. Later, that Friday night, I had a nightmare - I was soaring in the vivid blue sky like a bird. Then, I tumbled out of control as if I had been hit by something in midair. In a free fall, I awoke suddenly before hitting ground.

Frantic and afraid, I thought, "What was the meaning of this?". The dream was so vivid that, even now, nineteen years later, my recall is very clear, and I still have that unsettling - and haunting - feeling. I buried the nightmare deep within my soul and went back to sleep. I woke up the next morning, excited about hosting a BBQ for a small group of friends.

We were in the backyard, gathered around the pool when my cell phone rang. I went into the garage for quiet. It was a man's voice, and he gave me his name, explaining he was Tiffany's friend and coworker. He said he got my number from her cell phone and he proceeded to tell me Tiffany had been in the hospital all week, suffering post-op complications from her appendix surgery.

Then, he dropped the biggest bomb of all - she had passed away on that Friday night! I now realized my experience was her spirit saying goodbye to me via the dream-turned-nightmare. He went on to tell me how much she enjoyed our friendship and how much she respected me. I thanked him and hung up. At the same time, my friend Charles "Chuck" walked in, and I gave him the news. Chuck had met her on a few occasions. We embraced each other and wept for a while. I understood why she lost her balance and had poor circulation in her feet.

Sometimes, life can be downright cruel. An "angel", mother, and friend is taken from the world at only twenty-seven, and I was dropped right back to feelings of despair and desolation - not sure I ever fully left it to begin with in the first place. But, her spirit will forever be with me, in part because she gave me hope and inspiration.

Between 1993 and 2000, I experienced the following life-changing events, circumstances, and situations:

- Deaths of both parents
- Move to Los Angeles
- Divorce after twenty-two years of marriage
- Tiffany's death
- Empty nest
- Career transition

The 1990's would prove to be the most challenging decade of my life thus far, and the second most meaningful from a personal development standpoint. ROCK BOTTOM is a (real) place, situation, condition and a decision. Money and material things can be lost and regained over and over again, but the loss of people is indeed permanent in the natural life.

When people die, you will not physically see them again (here). In divorce, its loss is that of love, family and the single unit as one. Everything is affected: Loss of security, finances, and companionship, as well as long-term history of memories, holidays together, and other special moments. Both are painful. No matter how well you may be doing financially, money can't replace love and relationships.

It was during times of grief and lost relationships, I realized my true wealth in this life is in my relationships and meaningful connections. I've made and lost money (and made it again), but my loving bonds remained, no matter the challenge or situation in life. The other lesson from my life's losses was learning to love myself. This is the ultimate love - one must have (self) love in order to give it. I found my true self and self-love at that place called ROCK BOTTOM. Out of tears, I became stronger and wiser in life, and I moved on. "What doesn't kill you will make you stronger" is so true! *What the hell/heck (WTH) happened* to my life? Count my blessings and *Keep moving forward*!

My beach ball challenges and issues, age 40 to 50:

- Self-pity
- Loss of Passion
- Need for Freedom
- Loss of Creativity
- Self-love

What I've learned about life's transitional challenges:

Relational Loss:

Don't take people for granted; they won't always be here. Tell people you love them first, often, and with eye contact; don't anticipate a response of " I love you too." All too often we say "I love you too" only as a response, which falls short of sincerity.

Seek professional counsel to address prolonged grief and feelings of abandonment. Socialization is critical after the loss of a loved one. During the initial stages of loss, people are eager to support; however, over time, that support may wain. That's when we need consistent friendship, companionship or just someone to listen to us. But also, lean your ears to your friends. When a friend experiences a loss, don't worry about having the right words. Sometimes, that person may just need someone to listen and hear his or her memories of the lost loved one. And, it's okay to just sit and cry with them.

Remember, the five stages of grief are:
- Denial and isolation
- Anger
- Bargaining
- Depression
- Acceptance

The only way through grief is with time. There are no shortcuts, but time and reconciliation are the great healers. Remember - and celebrate - the good experiences and times, leave the negative in the past, and move on. For every loss, there can be so much to gain when one uses one's pain to seek positive outcomes, forgiveness, creating an open heart and HOPE!

Focus on the positive memories and experiences, fill your heart with light, and any darkness will disappear over time. Keep on living!

Relational Loss Of The living:
We can become estranged from people whom we love and matter for a myriad of reasons; a falling out, disagreement, just lose touch, bad health or illness, depression or isolation, holding a grudge, embarrassment or unknown reasons. Estrangement and separation, no matter the reason, can create a void or empty space within us, that wants to be filled.

In my 50's, I realized, no matter how much we care about or love someone, there may come a time for separation. In my cases of estrangement, primarily from family or friends, it's been due to unreconciled disagreements or the pace the requirements of daily life. Days turn to weeks, to months, to years, and eventually people get accustomed to no contact...until there's a graduation, funeral, wedding or other special event that brings people together. Fact is, there will be people who you may share life's journey; then, for whatever reason, we separate at the proverbial fork in the road.

All relationships are not designed to go the distance. Others may experience a period of separation, then resume right where we left off. Emotions have varying degrees of impact, depending on the depth of the connection. I have relationships where we may not speak for months, or even years, then reconnect as if nothing had happened. We think about each other, but are fine with status quo. It's the relationship separations or estrangement based upon conflict, animosity, or disagreement that carry the emotional weight of much-needed reconciliation in one form or another.

I had a relationship with someone who I cared about, but we had a misunderstanding and parted ways. Later, I tried to mend the fence; however, the other person was not receptive to my efforts. BUT, *at least I tried*. Then, I made peace with things and moved on. Should he seek to reconcile with me in the future, my door is always open.

Family member separation can be the most traumatic and emotional, and often the most difficult to reach positive reconnection, especially when it's a parent, older sibling, close family friend, or family member. Often, when people are older, they may have a sense of seniority or superiority over the younger person - this may also be driven by ego. They may stall, consciously or subconsciously, resolution for reconnection for control purposes. "The older we get the more, immature we may become".

No matter the situation, if the person is important to you, you love and miss them. So, take the initiative for reconciliation and reconnection. If they reject you, stay positive, pray for them, and move on. But, your positive intention may reap immediate or, in the case of rejection, delayed reconnection. Be the bigger person.

Divorce:

Divorce can be one of the most traumatic events and transitions in life. Psychological, physical, and/or emotional (Mind-Body-Spirit) imbalance may result in long-term negative ramifications When these complications are beyond our understanding or ability to resolve, get professional counseling help. I recommend counseling for the entire family both before, during, and even after divorce. Depending on your spousal situation, post-divorce counseling is highly recommended. "Starting Over" from divorce is not terminal; you can - and will - recover over time.

Quality open communication could avoid many divorces, so be open and honest and discuss from the heart with your mate. If kids are involved, try not to let them see you argue or be angry with one another. Communicate your respective positions in a calm and non-emotional manner. Forgive yourself, then your ex-spouse, for your divorce. Step back, take a deep breath, relax, and be honest with yourself about your role in the divorce. Yes, you played a role. Hence, the need to forgive yourself. "Takes two to tango." Never ever say anything negative or blame your spouse to the kids, either before, during, or after divorce. This can impact - even destroy - a child's self-esteem.

Work on becoming friends, or at least friendly, with your ex-spouse, especially if kids are involved. **You are responsible for your own happiness.** Kids are happy if they see you happy. At the appropriate time in your kid's development, sit down and tell them you're sorry for the divorce and how it impacted their lives. This will have life-long benefit for your relationship with your kids, and they'll love and respect you for doing it. These lessons are both the result of my divorce, as well as counseling and seeking solutions for reconciliation. Breathe in, then let go - time is the great healer, no matter our age.

"Empty Nest" Syndrome:

"Empty Nest" Syndrome is the experience of living after your children leave home, and it can be a combination of many symptoms after the kids are out of the house. Emotions range from relief to loss or even depression. One of the most vulnerable times in a couple's relationship is when the "nest" is empty. For 18+ years, the "date nights" and relationship-investing activities, involved those around your children's activities, not an "on-purpose" relationship, "love-bank Deposits". You must plan events after kids leave the house. What do you do to fill the blank time and space previously filled by the kids?

Planning and coping with the kids moving out and on should start at least two years prior to the transition. Parents should know where their relationship stands with each other, for pre-planning and emotional management. The planning process helps "blunt", or minimize, potential trauma resulting from the familial shift. Plan *before* the actual shift happens: What is your new vision as a couple, without the kids? What activities or hobbies will you do, both together and as individuals? It's a great time to expand your horizons, explore, and discover.

Maintain a close and loving relationship with your spouse throughout your marriage. Identify problems in the relationship when they arise, then discuss them with open and honest intent for resolution. Give as much time and love to the relationship with your spouse as you give to the kids; then, by the time the kids are gone, you're not looking at your spouse as a stranger, or have given up on the relationship.

Managing and coping with the actual shift is different for every parent. I've heard parents jokingly say things like, "Good bye and have a nice life.", "Only come back to take care of us.", "Can't wait to convert the bedroom into an office (or gym).".
Others dread the day it happens, with feelings of loss, and even grief. When my wife and I drove our son to college, she became emotional and so did I, but in different ways. The reality of his absence became evident a few days after he was gone. I missed my boy, but he was happy, and we had to move on, raising his younger brother. Staying in contact via phone and email helped manage the absence. Over time, we come to accept a new normative.

The worst thing you can do is try and play catch up in a relationship after the kids are gone. It's difficult to bridge many years of neglect to each other when the house is empty. Focus on the friendship with your spouse.

Get counseling if there are issues. Celebrate your accomplishment of raising your kids with your spouse. Tell your spouse you love him/her and want a fresh new life as a couple. Preserve what's left in the love tank and build on it. Do whatever it takes to stay together. But, if that doesn't work, then you can have peace in knowing you did everything possible to save your marriage.

While living in California, I met a man to discuss renting his home (we'll call him Bill). Bill was in his early 50's, and had been married for 25 years. We started discussing marriage and family, when a visible sadness came over him, then he began to tell me about his marriage and divorce. He and his former wife had two daughters in their early 20's. When I ask what happened to lead to divorce, he stated "I thought we had a great marriage, then one day she just left me without explanation!"

He went on to state that was why he was renting his home, he did not want to live there any longer without his wife. Clearly, he was devastated, and this was a relatively recent event. She had left with no reason or explanation, estranging herself from their two daughters in the process. He stated his daughters were angry and bewildered, rallying to support their dad. He never saw it coming, never seeing or recognizing the early indicators that his marriage had problems. Once the nest was empty, she wanted out! I saw Bill one last time several months later, and he nor his daughters had heard from her.

My friend of many years - I'll call him David - has been married for approximately twenty years, with two teenage sons. On the surface, his family is the ideal model of a happy and functional family. However, David and his wife are in their mid 50's, with one son graduating high school this year, and the second son graduating next year. However, he has shared with me, over the years, his unhappy marital situation. Their lives are totally focused on the kids and their careers, not each other.

He has mentioned he suspects, after the second son graduates from high school, the marriage might not survive. When I inquired as to why, he stated that there has not been any love between them for years, they are focused on their kids and the kids' future. I asked if he has communicated his true feelings, concerns and needs to his wife. His response, "No, we don't discuss those things." Then, I shared with him my own experience of empty nest, vulnerability, lack of communication, and eventual divorce.

I sensed he did not want to continue the discussion, so I ended the conversation with this statement, "Don't give up on your marriage without being open and honest about your feelings, and encouraging her to do the same." Consider marriage counseling NOW; don't wait until it's too late. Set new life goals together NOW, *before* the nest is empty.

Visit our website for feature blog post: *"The Boomerang Generation - Changing traditional empty nest norms"*.

Financial Shifts:

Save and invest your money - it should work for you, not the other way around. Cash and carry, use only credit that creates a healthy credit FICO score, then pay it off early. Long-term satisfaction versus short-term gratification - live below your means and look for bargains; see it as a challenge you can easily overcome. Save your money, sacrifice the material stuff, after 50 get debt-free, and focus on leveraging your income for long-term freedom and security. Consider attending Dave Ramsey - Financial Peace University. Go to www.over50startingover.net for additional resources.

Overall, I've Learned:

Humility, gratitude, and self-inspection, have a way of elevating us to a higher place. In my 50's, I become the person that I should have been all of my life, by addressing my beach ball issues and other unresolved problems. I am convinced, from here forward, the power of positive thinking and intention towards others and life, will help to keep me young in spirit, and happy at heart, no matter the trials and tribulations that may come.

Passion is a fuse that should always be lit. When it's out, we know something is missing; however, when it's lit, we truly can passionately move through anything. plan for the worst, and look for the good, but always expect the best. Stay focused on the "big rocks" of life and the "small rocks" will find their place. Mind-Body-Spirit are now in balance, and I'm in control of my destiny and legacy.

Deanna's Encouraging Wisdom

Max's life's experiences represents so many transitions for us. His journey embarks on change, loss, and heartbreak which leads to finding his passion and then ultimately transforming to a quality, healthy and joyful life.

I have friends in the midst of empty nesting. When their life had been hectically busy for 15+ years and revolved around kids' activities. Football games, dance recitals, practices, all kinds of school and church activities. When our children get in high school it really gets fun. Friday nights (especially in Texas) is filled with football games and band events. We were 'on purpose' for dinner before the football games during that season, we were chaperoning together, etc. Our schedules were full of fun, fellowship with each other, and we socialized with friends that had similar schedules. Then, all of a sudden, our last 'baby' graduates and leaves for college. YIKES! Now what are we supposed to do?

The house gets so quiet, so quickly! Quite possibly past conversations could have been made up of subjects about the children, exclusively! If we do not make it a priority to schedule things together with our significant other, then our enemy will likely take up the slack! I encourage anyone reading this now that is married or in a committed relationship to be on purpose with dating each other. Look forward to the empty nest and enjoy it while you can (some of us are experiencing the boomerang kids!).

I also have friends that have been through divorce that, unlike Max, are not friends with their ex-spouse. Those transitions can take such a toll on the core family and be an uphill battle to find not only the 'new normal', but the 'new joyful'. Single parents also have transitions that are unique and can be overwhelming later in life. All the more reason to arm yourself with practical tools to use to get you through these life's challenges with less pain and more prospective.

Let's move on – hopefully, you have something (or maybe multiple ideas) where you can go from here. I know Max's story is so inspirational, and I often comment, "If Max Gilreath can turn it around and 'Start Over' finding his passion and new life, then *so can you*!"

Now, it's essential to talk about balance in life. When we do identify our passion, and subsequently run fast and hard after it, we need to keep in mind as fun and enjoyable our workday has become, we have to continuously remind ourselves of our "WHY". The best way to start this process is asking yourself how you would like to be remembered. The core of our lives centers solely around relationships. Who do you want to be most proud of you? Whose appreciation do you most covet? What do you exchange your paycheck for (time, money, benefits, etc.)? I call that transaction your "currency".

There are different components to life balance: Your career, your family, your social needs, your physical health, your spiritual and personal development, and your financial well-being. First, to take care of others, we must ensure we take care of ourselves. I like to say, "Put *your* oxygen mask on first." To validate you are on track to take care of others, let's assess how well *your* crucial needs are being met. It is the easiest way to know you are taking care of yourself. Everyone has 7-8 crucial needs.

To get started, determine your "Top 3" from the following list and determine how (if) these crucial need are being met: Later, you will expand to ideally identifying 7-8 of your crucial needs.

- Approval and acceptance - From family, friends, peers, upper management, clients, etc.

- Time alone - Quiet time for Bible study, or journaling, or meditation. Just a few moments to yourself without interruption, preferably home alone.

- Exercise - Daily need for scheduled activity (90% of the benefit of exercise is above the shoulders).

- Unscheduled time – Spontaneity, especially if you do not like the pressure of constantly being overbooked and having a routine you have to follow daily, or if you like to take on many projects, or, perhaps, have a hard time with saying no, one of your crucial needs would be to schedule unscheduled time.

- Scheduled time - Easy to do Monday – Friday; however, if you have to also have structured time on the weekends and planned out months/years, then this is very likely an important need.

- Financial security - Knowing the checkbook has a positive balance and all (financial) responsibilities are met. Do you love to see surpluses in the checkbook, or are you thrifty, etc. You'll know if this is one of your crucial needs if life is in turmoil due to finances, but when the balance sheet looks good, you are in your groove.

- Socially motivated - High desire to be with people, enjoy social events, and place high value on group relationships, then maybe you're life of the party always wanting to invite more.

- Personal relationships - One-on-one time with those close to you, would prefer to go out with just one person, not a big fan of crowds (or always inviting more).

- Inquisitiveness - You always have to be learning something new, reading books, researching, and/or pursuing higher education.

- Competition - Keeps score, loves playing games, high need for challenges from self as well as others.

- Contribution - Needs to give or do for others, loves to volunteer, and helps out family, community and church.

- Empathetic - Being understood, important to you to be heard.

- Anticipation - Event planning, loves to plan each detail, loves Christmas, holidays, birthdays and surprises.

- Variety - Travels somewhere new, moves often, tries new things, high need for new surroundings.

- Projects - Always having new projects or missions; once you finish one, you need to start the next.

- Touch We all know a hugger, with the need for human interaction and physical touch; loves lap dogs and cats.

- Sleep - You need your sleep; if the necessary amount is not achieved, your whole day can be off.

- <u>Recognition for achievement</u> - Getting credit for ideas, feeling special and unique.

- <u>Order</u> – Goal-setter, loves order, and finds it hard to function in clutter or chaos. Prefers predictability and project timelines. Task oriented.

- <u>Music</u> - It is part of your every day, always listening, a must-have going on, even if it's only in the background.

- <u>Spiritual</u> - The daily need for prayer and meditation and the requirement to spend time with like-minded people.

- <u>Territorial</u> - Must have a physical space of your own.

- <u>Humor</u> - Always searching for that next laugh.

The stress that derives from not getting your crucial needs met manifests in many unbecoming ways. It is vital to determine all seven to eight of your crucial needs and communicate them to those close to you.

Interestingly, after identifying your needs, you will see how many on your list takes another person or people to fulfill it. You will need discernment to know who to go to for it, and, more importantly, who *not* to go to for fulfillment. Once your needs are being met, you will easily see and respond to those around you as to how you can help fulfill their needs. Just remember, "Put *your* oxygen mask on first."

Ultimately, job and life satisfaction has much to do with how your crucial needs are being met at home and especially at work. You will see the different personalities played out in these needs and how a perfect job match is so very important to joy-filled, purposeful careers.

Exercise:
Identify 7-8 crucial needs and **communicate them with those close to you**.

1._____

2._____

3._____

4._____

5._____

6._____

7._____

8._____

"Instead of saying, "I'm damaged, I'm broken, I have trust issues" say "I'm healing, I'm rediscovering myself, I'm starting over." - Horacio Jones

CHAPTER SEVEN

Real Change
Starting to Get It

Last Free Exit, or It Takes a Toll

"How you see your future is much more important than what has happened in the past." - Zig Ziglar

Our past should be viewed as a point of reference of the good, bad, and ugly, not as a predictor for our here and now or our future. Life's growth and development should never stop, no matter our age, circumstance, or position in life's journey. There are three predominant "sayings" I've found to be both accurate and measurable for me:
1. What doesn't kill you only makes you stronger
2. Everything happens for a reason
3. We all have an individual time table for learning life's lessons

In 1999, launching a privately-held consulting business as principal owner, I had the motivation and gravitational pull to create my own brand. I named it Max-I-Mize Consulting Services. Our targeted clientele was small to medium-sized IT telecommunications equipment and service providers, in the start-up and early-staged development. Our value proposition was: A.) Strategy and core business growth, B.) Operations, and C.) Brand innovation positioning for venture capital investment.

Consulting led to an offer to develop and lead a newly-formed business division for a well-established, small, privately-held mobility services company. From there, along with the company's VP for Engineering, we spun off a company focused on in-building distributed antenna systems, cell site engineering, outside plant, and utility coordination. We were developing the business while self-funding and seeking investment capital and/or venture capital.

However, after the events of 9/11, investment capital for IT-based start-ups all but dried up! My partner's personal asset liquidity was greater than that of mine, especially after more than a two-year "cash-burn" without any cash returns. So, we severed the business partnership. It was a very tough decision after a great deal of hard work and dedication, but it made good business sense for my partner to become sole owner while I went back to corporate. The company we founded together subsequently became AT&T's Minority Supplier for the year. My partner worked very hard and deserves the success that has endured for more than sixteen years.

That same year, my oldest sibling, James, died from cancer, at only sixty-two. He had retired from work at sixty to enjoy golf and boating. In my youth, I learned so much from James about life and living. While the age of 62 is far too young to die, he had a vision and plan for his retirement, though his life was cut short. I loved my brother and miss him dearly; however, I am enriched for knowing him in life, and learning from both his life and early death.

With resigned acceptance, in 2003, I moved back to Houston from Los Angeles. My motivation was to accept a new job opportunity. Jobs in IT Sales were very scarce after the ".com" tech failure and 9/11 disaster. However, I accepted my situation and moved back to Houston. Both Houston and I had changed over the ten years I lived in Los Angeles. Now, single, an "empty nester", and approaching fifty, I sensed a real change in my life, one more focused on reconciliation, meaning, and legacy. The job position was several levels below my experience, qualifications, and compensation expectations. But, it was a job in my field of expertise, and I needed one.

"Starting Over" in Corporate America was very difficult, especially after having owned and operated my own business. After swallowing my pride and checking my ego at the door, I moved forward with positive outlook. I wanted to buy a nice home and be able to share it with family and friends.

That same year, my dear friend, Daryl, passed away at only fifty-two from cancer. He was a good man, and I learned much from his integrity and standards.

My gains and losses in life helped create scaffolding for change.

Divorce has a way of fragmenting, and even breaking up, relationships within the realms of family and friends. My priority was to focus first on rebuilding and healing my relationship with my sons, Jay and Jody. While it took a lot of humility, open vulnerability, love, and faith, within three years of moving back to Houston, my interactions, especially those with my sons, were healing and becoming positive. Also, within a few years, I bought a beautiful home in downtown Houston where I spent quality time with family and friends.

Turning 50 was an amazingly uneventful, without dread or apprehension. One friend, who was already the big 5 0, said to me, "At fifty, it's all downhill. You can see the end." While I certainly understood my biological clock was ticking down, and I probably had more years behind than years ahead, I did not (and still don't) agree with the "downhill" philosophy.

Needs and Wants, Age 50:
- Meaning
- New horizons
- Healthy relationships

Though I continued life in the direction of acquisition mode, my passion for financial and material gain was waning. I wanted - and needed - more meaning in my life. While growing up in North Carolina, two of my six brothers were very musical. One was a singer and another played trumpet - they were involved in different R&B, Soul, Gospel, and Rock music bands in the 60's and 70's. At fourteen, I joined their R&B band as a "sidekick" and back-up singer. We had a lot of fun, but being in a band was lots of work with all the rehearsals, booking gigs, travel, set-up, and breakdown for the gigs, not to mention getting home in the wee hours of the morning.

I hadn't thought about singing or the band thing for over thirty years; however, when I turned fifty, I had an insatiable need to sing. So, I bought a high quality microphone with an amplifier and some mixing equipment, and I began rehearsing in my living room. I sang for family and friends and performed with bands whenever they'd allow me to sit in with them. Then, in 2007, I gathered up enough confidence to form my own band.

I had a deep-seated desire and need to act on some of my early life's dreams and passions. So, fortunately, I did not second guess my opportunity. When we take action towards our dreams driven by passion, somehow things fall into place. It's as though God had positioned people, situations, and resources to make it happen. God was waiting on me to make a decision and have faith for positive outcomes. Here's an example: Within only a few months of forming the band, I was able to attract some of the city's most talented musicians and singers. The word got out we had a very talented and good band.

WOW! This was the power of having a vision and moving forward, no matter the obstacles, and there were many, but I had taken a vision and concept and made it into a reality. You may have dreams and passions, from years past, that you gave up on or filed away for a more opportune time. Life's priorities for others, i.e. family and career, may dominate deeply personal, and individual, dreams and passions. However, the beach ball and its effects are waiting to be released so you can take action, because you can't take positive action until you've release all that negativity?! We all have an internal clock that says. "It's time." So, what are you waiting for? Make a decision, and, like me, you too can make your dreams and passions reality.

Within six months, we were out at clubs, performing live gigs. For the first year or so, I had a lot of fun. After all, I got into music for the love (and fun) of it. But then, the bloom fell off the rose. Booking gigs, rehearsals, musician egos, and the pervasive politics of the band entwined with business side of music became overwhelming. I worked a sixty-to-seventy-hour week while also putting in another twenty to thirty hours per week with the band, both as its manager and as its lead singer. I was no longer having fun. Exhausted, I decided to end the band experience. Yes, it was a difficult decision, but one that had to be made.

My interest in singing led me to writing and recording songs, providing a fun and creative outlet for my musical passion. In 2012, I decided to enter "The Voice" show auditions in Los Angeles, California. Participating in the audition process was a very exciting and fulfilling experience. There were thousands of audition participants whose average age was approximately twenty-five, and here I was, the "old guy" in the group at 56.

The audition process was segmented into groups, starting with approximately 250. Then, each group was divided into approximately 15 or 20 people. My assigned group included a couple of 17- and 19-year-old participants. Each one of us had less than a minute to sing (a cappella) to a single judge who probably wasn't more than twenty-two years old.

I delivered my song. When the audition was over, the 17-year-old young lady was selected to go to the next round. As we were walking out of the audition, one participant said to me, "I can't believe you were not selected!" That was all I needed to hear - validation for my talent from a peer. Sometimes, it takes just one stranger's support to encourage you forward.

"The Voice" audition gave me a heightened sense of confidence and relevance, two very important attributes that can diminish, or erode completely, over a lifetime. These are two of the biggest beach ball challenges. When we feel we've lost confidence and relevance, we start to build our own little cocoons. Add situational issues like divorce, job loss, empty nest, and financial reversals, and that cocoon gets wrapped tighter and tighter, until it starts to suffocate us.

We need to break free from that shell, take calculated risks, and embrace change. When we start to deal with these transitions, the tightly wound covering begins to loosen, and the layers of old wrap start to fall away. It is a tragedy to leave this life unfulfilled, without passion for life and living. The fact my father had so many talents that were unexplored due to lack of opportunity has fueled my passions to use and explore all of my talents. I had the opportunity and resources to do so, therefore I did. I once read "it's a sin to waste talent", and I believe this to be true. When I die, I want an empty bank account and a full soul, with the satisfaction of knowing I tried!

Over the years, I've had many conversations with family, friends, and colleagues about personal triumphs, trials, and tribulations of life. People with positive attitudes always talk about what they learned and have a great sense of humor. However, those with negative attitudes and worldviews, shared the following perspectives:

- **Blame** - is the loser's go-to alibi, the ultimate scapegoat, play-the-victim card for not accepting responsibility for one's actions, failings, or decisions. We raise our children to accept responsibility, understand right from wrong, and stand up for what's right. Then, when faced with matters of principle, so many people will take the easy way out.
- **Fear** - of "what if" - **F**eeding **E**very **A**nxiety as **R**eality
- **Regret** - Feeling sorry about what we did (or did not do)
- **Defeated** - Discouraged or beaten by a situation, event, or life
- **Self-pity** - Pity of one's self when we believe we are the victims of life's experiences; we also believe we've done nothing wrong, and therefore, somehow, deserve condolence.

This self-indulgent attitude is a very destructive behavior which may separate or distort personal reality. Self-pity is subtle in its self-absorbing approach to solving one's problems. When people are consumed with self-pity, the "woe-is-me" party, they tend to place blame for their problems or failings on others and not themselves.

The core issue with my own self-pity was not with placing blame, but rather in not accepting personal events and situations, reconciling them, and moving on. I did not realize, until years later, that I had not accepted the loss of my marriage and the deaths of people who I loved. This became very evident after the death of my brother Joe, "Chip", in 2009. I began drinking alcohol more and more, not working out, gaining weight, spending more and more time alone, experiencing insomnia and workaholic behaviors, with an overall sense of depression and sadness.

I was not fully aware of the effects of my own self-pity until 2012. Though very successful in my work and career, I increasingly began to lose my passion and enthusiasm for work. Working fifty to sixty hours per week with passion and enthusiasm is *very* different from putting in the same amount of time and effort without motivation.

Negative energy works against positive productivity

I had a new manager at work who had a hidden agenda to work me right out of the business. I became physically ill and emotionally drained, and eventually had to go out on disability.

When I returned to work, I was awarded President's Club Achievement for that year. Under the care of both a psychologist and medical doctor, I was now on the path of physical and emotional healing. However, still burned out with little left to offer my job, I began to work with Deanna to develop a plan for self-employment or finding the right career opportunity. My goal was to leave the company within a few months, even if I did not already have a job or self-employment in place.

Virtually debt-free and with money in the bank, I had little financial concern. What a blessing to receive full compensation and benefits for more than 6 months - I walked out of that office for the last time without regret and finally excited about my future!

During times of major transition, it's very important to fortify your "flanks" as insulation against negative personalities. Your *Life Team* can become your greatest asset. The following personalities feed-on the challenges, adversities, and challenges, even drama, of others.

Toxic Personalities
The Competitor and The Comparer

Positive attitude is not just "cliché"; it attacks the unexpected. For example, even in my most challenging life's situations, when I had positive thoughts about outcomes, usually a totally unexpected solution or opportunity would present itself. When I focused on the negative, I usually attracted negative outcomes, or worse, no outcome at all. Laws of attraction are always at work; however, after prolonged periods of challenge or life transitions, we can find ourselves in a slump, closed-minded, tired, and simply going through the motions of life, surviving and not living life completely.

I've learned to surround myself with positive and uplifting people. Enlightened people became so, by allowing and creating light in their life, and deflecting the dark. Over the past several years, I've noticed a subtle, and not-so-subtle, anger and anxiety in people of all ages. Negative people will go to extreme lengths to be right, so as to prove you wrong. Being right feeds their ego, while temporarily easing or filling their empty, internal spaces. Positive and secure people fill their own internal spaces with light and positive energy.

The Competitor: Many negative people are driven to compete against everyone. These personalities are opinionated, and everything is a debate with only one winner - themselves! They take what you know, combine it with what they know and now they know more than you and I. In an event where 99% of a situation can be positive, they'll focus on the 1% that's not. They have a way of extracting your positive energy, because of their inability to generate positive energy on their own.

They must win at everything no matter the costs. Don't share your vision dreams and ambitions with this personality type. They will find fault, say anything to discourage you, and only try to keep you "in your place", which, in their mind, is below themselves. Or, they'll just smile and won't say anything positive or encouraging. You are now a threat to their ego!

I'm learning to better manage and protect my personal relationships. By maintaining positive *Life Team* relationships, only with people who intentionally seek to generate positive outcomes and solutions, no matter the challenge or life transition. Positive energy and passion always wins, especially when we seek real and lasting change.

The Comparer: This is possibly the most cunning and calculating of the two personality traits. Why? Because their demeanor is more subtle and elusive. The *Competitor* is more direct, in your face and predictable, whereas the *Comparer* may lurk and observe, more than verbally communicate their thoughts. They compare their lives to others as a way to keep score; however, their envy, as with the *Competitor,* may evolve to in-your-face confrontation or the proverbial "knife in the back" tactics, especially if threatened by you. Both personalities' goal is to be one-up on you.

Perhaps you have these types in your life right now. Recognize anyone as either *The Competitor* or *The Comparer*?

During my early career years, I had a business mentor who taught me a very important "practice" for interacting with people. He said, "Don't discuss your personal finances (income) or class status with people outside your family, in casual conversation or with strangers. Your financial position or status is no one's business, and you open yourself to exposure to negative people (*The Competitor* or *The Comparer*)." Over the years, I've added two additional divisive topics to my list of guarded conversations: politics and religion. These three topics, money, politics, and religion, are "red-meat" for the *Competitor* and *Comparer*.

Influence versus affluence. Affluence is an abundant flow of supply, such as money or income, while influence is the power to affect, control, or manipulate something or someone. The key difference is power!

I have known and met many influential and affluent people over the past several years, primarily between Central and North America. In most cases, more influential people than affluent ones tend to exhibit both the *Competitor* and *Comparer* personality traits. The influential tend to compare and complete while on their quest for affluence. Many flaunt their economic and/or social status and/or class, while the affluent tend to be secure and confident in their standing, without the need for arrogance or narcissism.

I've had many experiences where an affluent or pretending to be affluent person would tell me the amount of money he or she earn, job title, value of their home, kids in private school, boat owner, country club membership, type of vehicle(s), etc. I never respond to counter their list of status inventory. Why? Because it's a tactic to get you to compare their position in life to yours. By not responding, they usually assume you're not at their economic level. Knowing that what I own, or how much money I make is none of their business, and I could care less about their socio-economic status. What they won't tell you, is that their usually in debt up to their ears. Men age 50 to 70 tend to be the most outspoken and arrogant, much more so than women.

I view both personalities as high **D**ominant, with a blend of Stable and Compliant for the affluent, and a blend of **I**nfluent and **C**ompliant for the Influential personality. My opinion is not based on evidence-based data, rather my personal observation and experiences. As I've matured and aged,

I have less to no tolerance for personality flaws. Competing and comparing with people does not lend value to a bigger purpose and meaningful life. Maybe you've had similar experiences? Take some time to think about that now.

Career Change - Job Loss and Transition

Change simply means "to make different." Don't be too proud to ask for help. In today's world, things are dynamic, and changes take place very quickly. A friend once shared with me this analogy about change: "Some people are still waiting for a locomotive train at the station, when a bullet train had already come and gone!"

Having worked for the same company for more than ten years, I had no idea how much the job market had changed. Plus, by then, I was a 56-year-old. However, I've always had the instinct and ability to embrace change, and, in my younger years, even led and created the change paradigm.

Decision drives change. I wanted and needed to change; however, I was mentally out of sync for making a definitive decision to do anything. I feared making the wrong decision, especially the implications of age and race discrimination. I gave myself permission to change, *but* I needed guidance as a starting point, with an out-of-the-box approach for creating and navigating a new life direction.

I reached out to Deanna because I trusted and respected her, both as a friend and professional. She was, and still is, a progressive, innovative thinker. If anyone could re-educate, remake, and reintroduce me for the new job market, it would be Deanna. My passion and enthusiasm were high, and I was extremely motivated for my next career opportunity. After several consultations, the two most critical questions she asked me were: 1.) What do you want to do? and 2.) Why? Her approach inverted my thought processes and turned me inside out...in a good way.

However, though I listened to her coaching intently, there was still part of me which resisted her approach. It was ego, and I had just enough of it to be dangerous, as in blowing an interview despite being properly positioned. I went to an interview partially prepared and armed with the new approach and technique; but, on the other hand, I wanted to take the old-school approach that had worked for me so well in the past. By the end, I knew I had blown it! Driving home, I critiqued my performance, and, now clearly understood had I followed the "new school" plan, I would have aced the interview. Lesson learned. It's a new job market, and I had better get with this program and get on that "bullet train."

Some of the techniques I used over ten years earlier to get the previous job were no longer effective in today's market. This was a real blow to my ego and confidence; however, with an attitude adjustment and willingness to change, I quickly made the necessary revisions and moved forward.

So many people go through life hanging onto yesterday and what use to be. Two particularly consistent ways to determine how well we embrace change are in our appearance: 1.) Our hair and 2.) Our clothing. Interestingly, many people tend to stall, or stop altogether, their progression in hair and/or clothing style at a point in time when they were the happiest or had the most fun in life.

I've seen people who are over 50 and have very youthful face &/or body; however, the 80s hair and clothing styles were a dead give-away. The goal is not to look like you're 20 again, but rather to be up-to-date and in the here and now. Appearance is a key indicator to an employer as to whether or not you or I can represent the company and its corporate image appropriately.

Finally, I totally bought into Deanna's coaching and began to adopt - and even enjoy - the growth and transformation process as she helped me to refocus on my value and worth. Now that my focus on the right job with the right company was clear and defined, I started "nailing" first interviews and getting call-backs for second and third interviews. More importantly , good-for-me career opportunities started coming my way.

The difference in my performance was the ability to execute the new paradigm with fresh strategies and different tools. The transformation and change got results. Passion, enthusiasm, and likeability garnered job offers. From the time I was laid off in April 2014 until I got the *right* job offer, it took seven months. It is a process, but I received the offer in November 2014, with a January 2015 start date.

The beach ball was on the surface, and my passion and my energy were high. At 57-years-old, I was ready for a new job in a new industry. This position was well below my experience and capability; however, I no longer had interest in climbing the corporate ladder or acquiring fancy titles. Now, my goal was to work hard while having fun, learning a totally new industry while making enough money to achieve my financial goals of achieving my retirement dreams.

I genuinely respected and liked the people and culture of this company. This was the second smallest business in gross revenues I worked for in my sales career; however, I *relished* the opportunity to work for a small, privately-held company. It had been many years since I felt that "fire in the belly"! I seized the opportunity to stop holding the entrepreneurial "beach ball" underwater, and I thought a smaller, private company with an entrepreneurial business spirit would be a good fit for my innovative approach and style.

Once I started with the company, I attacked my work with passion and vigor. I created a business plan with the engaged collaboration, support, and alignment of management, leadership, and cross-functional teams and personnel. I quickly developed a sales funnel and began to establish my value and worth, both within the company and with our customer base and prospective customer targets.

Within months of my hire, the manager who hired me left the company. This was a real surprise, and I became concerned about who would replace him. In professional sales, more often than not, when new sales management (Manager, Director, and VP) come on board, they seek to hire their own people from previous companies. And, if you were not their hire, you may be targeted for replacement. Unfortunately, from the time that new manager came aboard, I knew my days were numbered with the company.

My instincts were correct, and after reporting to him for approximately seven months, he fired me. The reason given was poor performance; however, it was quite clearly retaliation, based upon his once-hidden agenda to bring in someone of his choosing. I had worked for the company for sixteen months with a seemingly bright future. But, the universe had other plans for me (and my destiny). The day I was fired and the day I was laid off from the previous company, I had two very similar emotional responses: A.) Surprise, and B.) Relief and joy!

When I called Deanna with the news, we laughed and discussed the details and concluded it was time for me to *totally unleash* my passion and my potential for what I really wanted to do with my life, control my destiny, and be truly "forever happy"!!!

I knew in my heart I was being led to the next (higher) level of my life, not just bound for bigger and better things, but also a bigger and better me in Mind-Body-Spirit. Just like when I was laid off, it took me a few days to process, grieve, and define the emotional stuff before focusing on my next steps. Then, I immediately started to look for another job; however, unlike when I was laid off, I had a deep awareness of my Mind-Body-Spiritual health...and the fact I was unhealthy in nearly all aspects. I had gone to my doctor only a few weeks before I left the company, and he counseled me about the effects of alcohol and cigar smoking on my health and suggested I minimize or quit consumption of both toxins.

In truth, he had previously counseled me on several visits about the ravages of these substances, primarily to my blood pressure, kidney and liver function, and prostate issues. But, really, I hadn't been ready to hear it until I was on my way to Los Angeles to explore job possibilities and take my grandkids for a few days of vacation.

It was Thursday morning, approximately 9:00AM, and I had to stop at a well known copy store. I sat down, feeling nauseous. Sweating, I stood up to go to the restroom. When I awoke, I was on my back on the floor. There were four or five people standing over me - apparently, I fainted! One moment, I'm on my way to the restroom, and the next, I'm looking up at strangers, they were asking me questions, like "Sir, are you okay? Are you okay, sir? Do you know what happened?" One of the ladies said, "Sir, you passed out, and we've called the EMTs. They asked if you had an emergency contact for them to call."

If you've ever fainted or passed out, then you know what a weird and uncomfortable feeling it is when you wake up. I was in a total fog and completely dazed, just starting to process what had happened. I felt something wet on my face. It was blood from where my head hit the wall and opened a hole in both the wall and my left cheek. The emergency medics arrived and checked my vital signs, heart rate, and pulse. Then, they took my blood pressure. Their primary concern was I might have a possible concussion, but there was no sign of that. Still, my blood pressure was very high. However, since there was no concussion, I did not have to go to the hospital. So, I called my son to pick me up. I felt horrible and was unable to drive to the airport, so I considered cancelling my trip. But, I did not want to disappointment my grandkids or reschedule my job search. Fortunately, I decided to still go. So, bandaged and bruised, I was back on my way, headed to Los Angeles.

All I could think about on the flight was my doctor's warnings about making lifestyle changes to improve my health. The fainting spell was my "wake-up call", and I answered immediately with a decision and plan for change. Deanna's coaching awakened new sense of confidence and self-esteem, to accept my new and transformed "now". Transition leads to transformation - we just need to open our minds and hearts and be willing to try.

What I Learned:

My career had served its purpose: I was forced out of my comfort zone, pushed to move on to a bigger life. The importance of seeking help, such as career transition coaching, can be an invaluable resource to assist you, with retooling for your dream job or alternative career. Gratitude makes sense of our past while moving forward makes it worth it. Remember: Life's past dreams and passions have no expiration date.

Transitions are teachers in the classrooms of life, and we graduate better equipped to handle the next one. There is opportunity in the storm - just look and you'll find it. Beach ball challenges are opportunities for growth and fulfillment. Transition is the door to transformation, from pain to opportunity.

> *"The body keeps detailed records of its owner's abuse and neglect!"* - Max Gilreath

Things to Consider:

What is holding you back (beach ball) from living your dreams and passions? As I discovered in my life, *I was my own problem* for resisting too long to change, for waiting to let go of the past and embrace the future.

Write down any obstacles or challenges preventing you from living your dreams and passions. Followed by what you need to change in order to live a purpose and meaningful life, driven by dreams and passions.

_____

_____

_____

_____

_____

_____

_____

Deanna's Coaching Progress Through the Pain

The loss of a job or career does not compare to the loss of a loved one. Losing someone you have been close to has a whole different "Starting Over" playbook. But, it is part of what makes us who we are and molds us into who we become. It seems like when we lose loved ones, we look at ourselves and our current situation with "a new pair of glasses", one with weird magnification and a new sense of urgency for where we *are* as well as where it is we *want to be*. I often use this "new glasses" analogy in coaching.

At this point in our life, we are likely set in our ways. But, let's be adventurous, and dare to dream differently, uninhibited. For this exercise, we are going to look behind us in our past. As we process loss and change, it is vital we acknowledge the fact God has "allowed" all of our hurts and transgressions, to be later utilized for His good and His glory. He never wastes a hurt. Trust the timing of your life.

Keeping in mind, if our God were small enough to be understood, He wouldn't be grand enough to worship. Here is the visual which always helps me put these things into perspective: I imagine our enemy required to approach the sovereign and holy throne of God and ask permission to sift His beloved (you or me). Sometimes, in the events of our lives that are painful, etc., He said, "Yes." But, I also like to remind myself and you, there are many times our enemy approaches His throne, and God says, "NO!"

When we look back at the valleys of our lives, with "a new pair of glasses", we can often see the sanctification process that was on-purpose, by a loving God to give us the experiences necessary to live out His plan for our lives. Remember: He never wastes a hurt! Again, trust the timing of your life.

In my case, I thought I would retire at the telecommunications company I worked for. I loved my job and loved the company brand and culture...until change came. Mergers, downsizing, etc. I was miserable *for 2 years* before I finally woke up and said, "I don't know what I am going to do, but I know what I am *not* going to do for one more day!"

Even in those dark two years, God was preparing me to truly understand and relate to my future clients. He guided me through tough situations and terrible struggles - all so I could have the first-hand knowledge and experience to truly empathize with, and be a testimony to, those who find themselves going through a career transition later in life. Like Max has demonstrated by his transparency and forthrightness, let's inventory the valleys in your life that, when you look back now with "a new set of glasses", you can see the hurts were to prepare you for something bigger, more meaningful - and if you had not had to go through those tough situations, you would not have the valuable first-hand knowledge you have today. You could have never treasured that view from the mountaintop had it not first come from the view of the valley.

God loves us too much to let us develop naturally. What we learn in the darkness are "forever lessons". It is so empowering to know something good and tangible can come of such loss. I am sincerely amazed and in awe of the many examples God has given me as to how the loss of a job or career can transform into a dream vocation, where if change were not forced, it would have never been uncovered, remaining potential unfulfilled.

Proverbs 19:21 - You can make many plans, but the Lord's purpose will prevail. (NLT)

Don't you love it when we seem to help God along in *our* path to a joy-filled and purpose-driven life? If you really, really want to know what it is that would give you great satisfaction, wealth, and a servant-heart that overflows with energy and passion, ask your Creator. He authored our lives, and He knows us better than we know ourselves because He is *The One* with the plans and the "blueprints" to where He wants us to be (which, I assure you, is a much better place and situation than we could *EVER* dream up for ourselves!). Trust in the divine.

What has He been telling you through job loss, health concerns, or unpleasant experiences? I try to embrace the fact that God never wastes a hurt, so when we do allow reflection, let's see if we can uncover His "love lessons" and apply them. Think of them as your "blueprint". It may not illuminate exactly what to do, but more often than not, it will outline exactly what *not* to do (again).

One thing that breaks my heart is when I come across people who have invested many years in a company and had their mind set on retirement from that company. Never in their wildest dreams did they think of finding another job or getting laid off. Yet, I have experienced this, my husband has experienced this, and many clients "Over 50" have experienced this. It comes back to me thinking we have/had it all figured out, then God says, "Really? Really, Deanna?" At first glance, we are devastated, perplexed, scared, and, overall, NOT HAPPY! I especially have compassion for those who have invested 20, 25, 30+ years and are let go abruptly when they still have so much more to contribute and accomplish. Then, add on the fact that the timeline of these changes typically comes with other transitions that are going on, like funding college for our children, empty nesting, and taking care of aging parents. Now, we must add financial setbacks to the list.

Many have planned for emergency funds, which sustain us for six months to a year or more. But, where did we plan for our career to come to a screeching halt when we have not had to enter the workforce and compete with younger candidates since the 1990's? I remind myself often, and would like to share with you - the will of our God will not take you where the grace of God won't sustain you.

Believe BIG, Pray BOLD!

CHAPTER EIGHT

*Awakening Within
Integral Design*

Mind-Body-Spirit are Integral

*"When wealth is lost, nothing is lost; when health is lost,
something is lost; when character is lost, all is lost."*
- Billy Graham

Good health is the foundation of human life. It includes physical fitness, mental health, and social well being. We can be unhealthy, even in the absence of infirmity. Healthy socialization "Over 50" leads to a better quality of life. Interaction with others, when combined with physical exercise, meditation or prayer, healthy diet and positive outlook, promote integral and sustainable wellbeing. Reimagining ourselves to be healthy and whole is the first step. Mind-Body-Spirit are integral, and when disconnected, cannot create optimal health benefits. During my few days in Los Angeles, I had time for deep soul-searching. The copy store event from Chapter 7 provided the wake-up call to stop and help me reverse my negative health direction.

So, I began putting together plans for healing my Mind-Body-Spirit. This was familiar ground for me because I've always had the innate sense of knowing when to take action, but it had been approximately fourteen years since I had to reconcile the Mind-Body-Spirit equation. Now, with imminent health concerns, thirty-plus pounds overweight, abusing alcohol and tobacco, and spiritually weak, it was time to act again.

No more delays or excuses - I went to the doctor for a complete health exam; then, immediately engaged the following Mind-Body-Spirit get-well plan. I waited too long to change my behaviors and lifestyle. I looked at my health situation as dire, and I knew what to do.

My decision to improve the quality of overall health started with creating a healthier mindset for change. My father would say, *"It all starts in the mind. Manage it and you'll live a healthy life."* For our purposes here, the *mind* is the element or complex of elements in an individual that feels, perceives, thinks, wills, and especially reasons.

I started my journey back to good health and well-being with reading and meditation. Reading health and fitness books and magazines, meditating and re-imaging (a mental representation of something previously perceived, in the absence of original stimulus). In other words, comparing the previous self to the person one wants to become. The person who I wanted to become led me to develop and embrace the following steps, for achieving integral good health.

1. **Mind:**
   - ❏ Meditation and Prayer
   - ❏ Re-imaging, mental view
   - ❏ Breathing exercises

- Minimize TV viewing to 1 or 2 hours daily
- Reading fiction, non-fiction, inspirational, motivational, etc. for personal growth and relaxation
- True Relaxation from your toes to your brain
- Rest

2. Body:

Focus on improved muscle strength, endurance, flexibility, and balance. Consider running/jogging and aquatic exercise to prevent the occurrence of arterial or other cardiovascular issues.
- Hot Yoga 5 days per week
- Swimming, running, walking
- Increase vitamin supplements (multiple with emphasis on Zinc, Magnesium and Vitamin D)
- At least 1 gallon of water and coconut water per day
- Detox from meats, red, poultry, pork, and fish
- Daily requirements for fiber, vegetables, and fruits

3. Spirit:
- Meditation and prayer
- Breathing exercises
- Reading inspiring and uplifting books
- Thought management
- Positive thinking
- Nature, camping, hiking, and spending time at the beach (or just outside). Nature has a calming effect bringing Mind-Body-Spirit together.

    I developed my daily plan, and re-engaged, reconnecting my life with my mind, my body, and my spirit. My father's examples about health and philosophy and general well-being became reminders for discipline and dedication to healthy living every day. I immediately reduced alcohol and tobacco consumption.

    Now, I've been virtually free from these beach ball behaviors, for more than a year. There is an occasional urge to smoke, more so than alcohol; however, all are within my control and without anxiety. The "natural high" derived from Hot Yoga and meditation, coupled with proper diet and the alcohol and tobacco detox, is such a gift! Putting one's Body-

Mind-Spirit in a state of good health is an indescribable feeling of rebirth, renewal, and re-creation – it gives everything new meaning. Everything really does happen for a reason, even being "fired". It's all in one's attitude and perspective.

As I began to intensify the effort, structure, and consistency of my exercise and training, I started having physical challenges. I began experiencing chronic muscle strains in the lower calf muscles for both legs. Both my trainer and physical therapist (PT) could not explain why this was happening. Then, I spoke with my son, "Jay", who have extensive experience and knowledge of sports anatomy. He thought the problem in my calves may be because of weakness in hamstring muscles, tendons, and ligaments.

I went back to my PT and shared my son's analysis. The therapist began trigger point (a tender area of a muscle that causes pain when over stimulated) massage for both my calf and hamstring muscles. He stated that my hamstring muscles were "extremely tight" affecting the lower calf muscle areas.

The following day, I had significant improvement in both calf muscles. Just needed to rest and allow the healing process to take hold. The weakness of my hamstrings were affecting the health of my lower calf muscles. Therefore, I began a fitness program, to strengthen my hamstrings, which would minimize or eliminate the chronic calf problems. *Weakness in one area affects another*. Mind-Body-Spirit are integral, and equal focus should be given to all three for optimum wellness.

"Man. Because he sacrifices his health to make money. Then he sacrifices money to recuperate his health. And then he is so anxious about the future that he does not enjoy the present; the result being that he does not live in the present or the future; he lives as if he's never going to die, and then he dies as if he never really lived."   - Dalai Lama

My beach ball included the following challenges:

- Bad Health and the road to recovery and wellness
- Passion - Wants & Needs
- Unhealthy habits
- Loss of self

For now, just write down your individual beach ball issues and challenges - you may just be surprised at what you've been suppressing and how it's been holding back your life.

_____

_____

_____

_____

_____

Everything in life is in a constant state of change. Watching my sons, Jay and Jody, grow up was a special experience. But, seeing my granddaughters, ages nine and five, grow up is the ultimate surreal experience. I think I'm more aware of my grandkids' evolution than my sons' because I'm older, less busy, and more focused on the "now" moment. I see them a few times per month, and I'm always amazed at the subtle changes in their appearances and personalities.

I recently drove by the home I bought in downtown Houston in 2006. Now, the neighborhood, and my old home, look and feel very different from when I lived there. Changing, evolving, repositioning, and moving. Just when we get comfortable, things change. It made me think of the book "Who Moved My Cheese?" by Spencer Johnson, M.D. Like my old neighborhood, the meanings of my beach ball have also changed as my life has progressed - my passions, needs, and wants have changed significantly in my 50's - from allowing my issues and challenges to control me, to controlling and eliminating them, allowing the real and authentic self to emerge.

I've changed and evolved - now, I have a deepening need for authenticity in my relationships and in my sense of self. Materialism and "things" matter less while intangibles, like joy and peace of mind, matter more. At this time, my focus is on simplicity, legacy, and the passions for being, not becoming. My desire now is for the inner, not outer, and for being, not becoming.

Currently, I have a fuller appreciation for the present with an aspiration for self-directed destiny. Now, I'm embracing, and even loving, change. I had been "in pursuit" for so long, I forgot what it meant and felt like just to "be". Sometimes, life's events and situations force us to explore the unexplored. This is a good thing - better late than never. Now, I'm on a good path, my on-purpose path, and I own it.

In the four months since my firing, I focused on finding a new career, my Mind-Body-Spiritual growth and development, and becoming more aware every day of the gradual change taking place within me. Know that being alone is not the same as being lonely.

Personal Treasure

Focus on the total "Micro" self, Mind-Body-Spirit
- Positive
- Sense of health and well-being
- More energy
- Passion, fire, and motivation
- Not stressed and anxious
- Creative
- Aware
- In the moment
- Calm
- Sleeping better

As I awakened and transformed into the new me, my intuition and instincts were vibrant and alive, and I was back in the pilot's seat, operating from a healthy place and the state of my authentic self. There was a very real paradigm shift happening this time. Unlike the last time when I was laid off with multiple job opportunities in hand, this time, the opportunities and employer interest were rare and limited, despite the US unemployment rate the lowest in many years. Regardless of my glowing track record of success, very little was happening.

However, the other major change that occurred was I wasn't concerned or worried because I had a sense of well-being and positive outlook, I knew in the deepest part of my soul, good things were ahead. Deanna coached me about both regaining my passion and confidence **and** taking my power back with a plan specifically tailored to ME, my passions, and my dreams. It was September, and I knew from experience if I did not have a job offer by November, chances were very low I would go back to work for a public, or even private, company the following year. Why? Because America is not an "Over 50"-friendly country, and companies have the ability to assess your age simply by your resume, LinkedIn profile, keywords, formatting, etc.

But, moving forward, I continued my job search and the development of my Mind-Body-Spirit while also acting on Deanna's direction and coaching. Transformation is a stage-based process with a beginning, middle, and *forever* – and here I was, in the middle stage of my transformation process, going deeper into the change with full awareness and completely open to the next level...whatever that may be.

Finding Self-love in Self-Reflection

A "mirror walk" is the walk of personal reflection based upon truth since the "mirror never lies". My "mirror walk" included taking a deep and closer look at my life, and was focused on my whole being, Mind-Body-Spirit health and rediscovering the real me, that had been lost and diminished over the years.

Aloneness, as defined by Psychology Dictionary.com, is the state of being alone or kept apart from others. Synonyms include: insulation, privacy, secluded, seclusion, segregation, separateness, solitude. Self-reflection is defined by (Psychology Dictionary) as the examination and contemplation of our thoughts and actions. It can also be known as "reflective consciousness". So, I entered a period of deep self-reflection, in solitude and aloneness, limiting distractions, taking my "mirror walk" just for me. We can all take the "mirror walk" for self-reflection and healthy growth.

It's been six years since my last meaningful relationship with a woman, but it's been a gradual and natural process that has also reduced the need or desire for that kind of meaningful relationship. After that last relationship was over, I knew I needed time alone to give me the opportunity to go deeper into myself. This was some of the most valuable and meaningful time of my life. Why? I realized I repeated a co-dependent pattern of rescue - trying to save people from themselves, while making me miserable in the process. Time alone allowed for the natural, organic, internal "mirror walk".

Growing up as a child in North Carolina, I loved the experience of spending time in the forests, where I could hear the concert of animals, birds, and insects communicating in a language quite indiscernible to the human ear, yet beautiful to the soul. Being alone allowed for a time of peace and serenity. Being alone in the spiritual and physical commune with nature and God. Being alone every once in awhile is good for the soul. I use this communing with nature as therapy – rest and respite from the rigors and noise of everyday life. In my aloneness, I have learned to be still in order to hear and listen to that inner voice.

Before this period, I handled aloneness as an unhealthy retreat to being lonely, as an organic or natural self-defense mechanism into the abyss of depression. Unresolved issues and unmet expectations are the emotional and physical albatross, slowing us down, holding us back, pushing us and our beach ball underwater, draining our passion and energy along the way. Many people are afraid to be alone, afraid to take the "mirror walk", afraid what they may find and see, what their inner voice may whisper, and what might be required for healing.

Understanding, acceptance, forgiveness, and renewal require effort, work, and maybe even professional help. I took the painful "mirror walk" because I was open and ready, mature enough to accept my mistakes, failings, and losses to arrive at "I AM OK" and ready to live at the next higher level. My personal garden has been "weeded", so now it's time to plant new seeds in the fertile soil of my refreshed "Mind-Body-Spirit" garden and let them grow. The inner voice led me to the beginnings of innermost peace with a happy, safe place in both my mind and my physical body reality. I also developed a mantra.

I AM THANKFUL FOR:
- ☺ Limitless Life
- ☺ Limitless Love
- ☺ Limitless Potential
- ☺ Limitless Energy
- ☺ Limitless Passion
- ☺ Limitless Desire
- ☺ Limitless Resources
- ☺ Limitless Gratitude
- ☺ NO LIMITATIONS OR LACK!

Funny how the things we hated in our youth, like gardening and farming, can come full circle to where we love them as we age. My brothers and I worked in the vegetable garden on our family farm, spending every spring and summer tilling, planting, and harvesting crops - everything from corn, to green beans, to tomatoes. It was approximately an acre, but when you're twelve, it seemed like 10 acres, and in the 90-plus-degree heat with no tractor or plow, it was all (hard) manual labor. But, I sure loved to eat the food it produced - one of my first opportunities to learn delayed gratification and savoring the fruits and vegetables of my labor.

In those days, freezers were considered an expensive luxury item. Therefore, my mother and her sisters canned our crops for many years. Ultimately, however, we got a freezer. In my 50's, I got the urge to garden again - there's something very spiritual and therapeutic about putting one's hands in dirt and planting the food you eventually eat.

The desire to garden again, coupled with my love for forest, water, and animals led me to visit Costa Rica, the number one eco-tourism destination in the world and only a 3-hour direct flight from Houston, Texas. I fell in love with the rainforest, beautiful beaches, and wonderful people. And, shortly thereafter, I purchased land for farming and as a family legacy. My aloneness provided a safe haven for internal optics, thought, and the stillness to listen - and hear - that inner voice, where I began to blossom and emerge anew.

Initially, I downsized from a large house to a two-bedroom apartment. Now, I have a one-bedroom apartment, which has given me a living environment of simplicity, only having what I truly need. At this point in my life, I no longer need the spoils of comfort. Getting to know who I really am as my most authentic self has given me a sense of freedom and renewed love of self.

My happy place now is in just being in my mind and in my imagination, visualizing the faces and smiles of my sons and granddaughters, visualizing our property in Costa Rica, and visualizing the images of future times and adventures together there. My safe place now is in prayer and meditation, in the sensation of every breath, and in the absence of anxiety and negative thoughts.

Comfort and success can become life-altering - a drain on passion and drive, with the extreme focus on "want" versus "need". If we are not careful with our inner spark, comfort can breed complacency and success can breed egotism. I lived both as they became life's residue. But, in my aloneness, I became strong again, hungry for meaning, ever grateful for all that life had given me, and thankful for the rediscovery and awareness of what was in me all along.

Self-Reflection Repositioned My "True North" Life's Compass

Self-pity and self-love cannot peacefully co-exist. Self-pity leads to comparing yourself to others and feeling sorry for yourself, wanting to reap benefits but makes excuses, while self-love says "I AM worthy". Love for one's self does not mean egoism, which is unhealthy. Make no mistake - egoism is pride in self and the absence of altruism, whereas altruism is selflessness in the principle of concern of the welfare of others. Self-love means having the courage to be genuine in this world. Love of self is *essential* to loving others. You cannot love others fully until you truly love yourself. Being alone helped to heal my wounded spirit. I began to forgive myself for not believing I was worthy of being happy and fulfilled. In my aloneness, in my stillness, I could hear God the Creator and the Source speak to my weary soul.

"Starting over is a blank canvas, using an old brush (experience) and fresh new paint and vibrant colors. COMPLETELY ALIVE *again*."
- Max Gilreath

Notes: What is your inner voice saying to you?

_____
_____
_____
_____
_____
_____
_____
_____

Transformation

Caterpillars of the Monarch butterfly change and transform into some of the most recognizable winged insects over a life-cycle period of three to six weeks, depending on the climate temperature. I've heard people refer to the caterpillar as an "ugly" creature. But, from my perspective, I disagree and view the caterpillar as "a work in progress" - not "ugly", but rather in stage of metamorphosis to becoming a beautiful butterfly. Transition, passion to transformation.

The "work in progress" caterpillar does not know it will become "beautiful" as a butterfly because it's continually in a state of being unaware of becoming. And, we humans go through a similar process of transformation.

The beauty stage of the caterpillar to butterfly transformation does not take place until late in the metamorphosis. This transition may also be analogous to human biological and chronological evolution. As humans, our (Western) society indoctrinates us with the belief youth is beauty and of high value while age and maturity are somehow ugly, lacking, and diminished in value. Western culture, especially, devalues age and maturity and experience while Eastern, African, and Latin cultures tend to revere these traits (age/maturity/experience), seeing as central to acquired wisdom, and, as such, are to be respected and edified.

My personal transformation is a story of "survive to thrive", 40 years of adult survival: Asleep then awake, unaware then aware, bad decisions then good ones, living and learning through all of life's experiences. In my life, one lesson will always stand out: The two-fold example of accepting and then letting go. Accepting what we do not control, and then letting go of the unhappy experiences are very important parts aspects of life and maturation.

However, we live in a blame-oriented society. It's so much easier - and expedient - to blame someone (or something) else for our problems, instead of accepting responsibility and accountability for our own actions, situations, and states of our personal life. The only legitimate victim is when one has no control over the act or action that creates negative outcome, such as abuse.

Yet, there can be no victimization when one *controls* the outcome. When blame replaces personal accountability, the blamer is weakened and diminished. Aware of change, and yet unaware, my life up to my 50's was spent focused on becoming something else or getting something new, in pursuit of one thing or another (mostly for career and financial gain), becoming versus being. A big part of my passion and joy is just being me, being in control of my beach ball. No one (or thing) can control our beach ball, nor should we let them. However, we relinquish control to people and things every day, and we are usually blindly unaware. We give external forces and stimuli power and control over our passion, energy, and joy, without even knowing we're doing it.

Which of the following do you allow?

- Fear
- Wrong job or career
- The bad marriage or relationship
- Control through money and materialism
- The boss who suppresses or diminishes your ability, talent, or success

These experiences feed and promote the "CWS" personality. Our challenge becomes making the once seemingly impossible both possible and real.

The beauty of age and maturity comes in wisdom, knowledge, understanding, and perseverance. Western cultures place more value in youthful looks, vibrant appearances, and the superficial. Unfortunately, so many people begin to lose their self-worth when youth turns to maturity. WAKE UP! If I did, anyone can. But, you can't transform into the beautiful butterfly you're meant to be until you take ownership of your "caterpillar" challenges and find your self-love. Either you own your beach ball, or someone else does. Either you control your beach ball, or it controls you.

I was unable to accept the losses in my life and end self-pity in my life until my 50's. Unable because I was unaware it existed. But, once aware, wisdom gave me the focus and courage to find resolution. Identifying the problem(s) and accepting responsibility are the two most difficult aspects of transformation because placing blame is the easy way out.

In my life of self-pity, I did not blame others; however, I did internalize my issues and blamed myself, which produced unhealthy and self-destructive behaviors, such as alcohol, tobacco, unhealthy diet, and lack of exercise. I am the perfect example of the Mind-Body-Spirit connection - first in an unhealthy way; then, as I changed my behaviors and attitudes for the better, in a more positive light. And, it was Deanna's coaching that helped to provide the roadmap for healing and resolution.

Over my life's journey, reading inspirational material played a key role in understanding and healing. I usually read two to four books per year and seek out motivational, how-to, novels, or spiritual subject matter based upon a specific challenge or situation I may be in. One thing all of my readings have in common is my search for answers. I rate "The Bible" as the top guidebook for my life's journey. Here are my Top Ten after "The Bible":

1. "7 Habits of Highly Effective People" - Stephen R. Covey
2. "Ageless Body Timeless Mind" - Deepak Chopra
3. "Your Instinct In Action" T.D. Jakes
4. "The Secret" - Rhonda Byrne
5. "Power of Intent" - Dr. Wayne Dyer
6. "Rich Dad Poor Dad" - Robert Kiyosaki
7. "Unlimited Power" - Tony Robbins
8. "Talent Is Never Enough" - John C. Maxwell
9. "You Are Not Your Mind" - Eckhart Tolle
10. "You Can, You Will" - Joel Osteen

Each of these books has provided answers and guidance over the years. Life is an accumulation of lessons, experiences, and outcomes. Being fifty (and beyond) is a great opportunity to put it all together, coupled with innovative resources, such as life and career coaching that add to your life's "success team". Otherwise, stagnation and "CWS" behavior can take root. If you're a reader, write down the names of the top books you've read over the years and why. If you're not a reader, write down other resources you've found helpful. This quick, little exercise will provide much-needed information for journaling later.

The Butterfly is designed to Fly – And, so are YOU!

Research shows it takes at least twenty-one days to form a habit. That's three whole weeks. And, from what I've read and heard for years, it takes at least that same amount of time to *break* a habit. I think ex-smokers, as a group, have great insight into this subject. As a cigar smoker for more than twenty years, and now ex-smoker, I can provide empirical evidence from personal experience, not clinically-based, controlled experiments or theory.

From the time I decided to stop smoking an average of seven cigars per day, to the time I no longer had the craving was approximately 90 days. However, to this day, there are triggers which cause my brain to say, "Just one more". I think chemical addictions and habits are as challenging, if not more so, as habits of learned behavior which is a response to stimuli.

My 50's have given me the opportunity to look back on my life, assess the good, bad, and ugly of my life's seasons and evolution. Stronger, wiser, and bolder, I made a clear and conscious decision to start my life over, to be happy, healthy, and passionate about my daily existence and meaning, which ultimately creates my legacy to myself, family, friends and the world. "Starting Over" in life means to let go of everything in the past that wasn't working and move on, to abandon or end, to begin again. The word "start" is a verb meaning to take ACTION or to ACT.

Why is it seemingly so different - and sometimes, difficult - to take action when we are "Over 50" versus our younger years? Here are a few possible explanations:
- Fear
- Excuses

- Sloth (mentally or physically)
- Ego
- Pride
- Shame
- Poor health
- Bad habits
- Indecision
- Perfectionism (or any "-ism")
- Loss of hope
- Negative attitude
- Hopelessness
- Depression
- Set in our ways
- Boredom
- Low self-esteem

In his "Summa Theologiae", Medieval theologian Thomas Aguinas said, "Sloth is sluggishness of the mind which neglects to begin good...it is evil in its effect, if it so oppresses man as to draw away entirely from good deeds." Sloth, also known as one of the seven deadly sins, is the avoidance of physical work or spiritual endeavors, which creates a weakened and sluggish Mind-Body-Spirit connection. The brain and spirit require exercise and regular usage the same as the physical body. I've known many "CWS" people over the years. Some were slothful in body while others were in mind and soul. And, many were slothful in all three areas: Mind-Body-Spirit.

Interestingly, most people I know in the Sloth, or "CWS", category have one thing in common: They have (or feel they have) few if any opportunities for cathartic, psychological relief through the open expression of strong emotions. This release of emotion causes a healing catharsis and goes back to the need for professional help, be it for the psychological, emotional, spiritual, or physical.

One can't effectively start over with unresolved "infrastructure" (our problems and repeated issues). We can put a "band-aid" on them, effectively glossing over them, making excuses, and deflecting for temporary relief, but eventually, our beach ball pops back to the surface. So, until our issues and challenges are dealt with at the "root", we cannot fully and completely "start over" as new beings. Instead of "flying" in life, we crawl slothfully along without passion and joy.

My father understood the travails of the sloth mentality and embraced the Mind-Body-Spirit approach to life. Always energetic and passionate, he loathed the slothful spirit in others, especially those of his "Over 50" generation. He would make comments to me like: *"That guy is always complaining. I can't stand to be around him." "He's an old man in his mind, not his body. Thus, his body is old also."*

My father understood the power of the mind, so he would say, *"Guard your mind. Be careful what you let into it."* He also practiced positive thinking, always greeting people with a hearty "Hello" or "How are you doing?", and always replying "I'm doing great!" To this day, more than forty years later, his words still hold true. He did not have the financial means to seek help for his issues; however, he unknowingly was cathartic in his emotional expressions, which reflected an inner pain. He was an organically brilliant man.

Whether you are miserable or passionate, life is about choices. No one can make that choice but you. And, *you* must own it, consequences and all. We like to hold everyone accountable but *ourselves*. Then, it seems accountability is optional. We put our love into others while our own "love tank" is low (or, worse, empty). To be selfless means to lose the ego, *not* your self-love.

What have you done in life to warrant regret and self-loathing? For me, it was divorce and what it did to my family and regret for other mistakes and decisions I made. Don't be that elephant tied to the stake, conditioned to believe others control his movement. "Over 50" provides a great opportunity to grow up, accept, reconcile, and move on. We can do little, if anything, about the past, but we can control our here and now. "Over 50, Starting Over" means you've made the decision that it's NOT OVER!

What I learned:

Through re-imaging for modeling and creating a better life, I rediscovered the real me, with a foundation of healthy Mind-Body-Spirit. I must love myself in order to love others. The power of self reflection, solitude and nature helped regain the power within me. Solitude can be healing. Being still, listening, and reflecting in order to create a happy and safe place within me. Take action, cancel the wake-up call before it happens.

Change before you have to, think about the long haul, 10, 20, 30 years or more, however many years that I have left I control the quality of my life, based upon my attitude and perspective. Positive thinking is also medicine, an elixir composed of uplifting and inspiring ingredients (your recipe). Balance, all things in moderation, and don't complain when life is not perfect. No one really cares about my complaints, and even negative people are drawn to positive energy. Minimize, or eliminate, alcohol and tobacco consumption. Minimize stress and anxiety - stop worrying - it's a waste of imagination. Create a healthy and integrated Mind-Body-Spirit lifestyle. Learn to be still and quiet through meditation, prayer, and breathing.

Be proactive with your health - many health challenges can be resolved, especially if addressed in early stages. Take charge of your health - read and research health concerns as well as health innovations and cures. No one should know more about your body than you.

Also, be open-minded to non-traditional health and wellness approaches - the human body is composed of the same minerals and vitamins as the earth, plants, fruits and vegetables and water. Eat foods with life, not ones that are already dead with no active nutrition value.

Sometimes, old-school cures and home remedies are better than taking a pill, so research the alternatives. Steer clear of salt, flour, and sugar - this is a daily vigil since practically every form of food source contains some form or variation of these killers. But, remember, you can't go wrong with living foods, such as vegetables, fruits, and fiber-based foods.

Get a minimum of 30 minutes of exercise daily, drink lots of water, and get daily exposure to sunlight. Go get an annual physical, do your "Over 50" screenings, and have your vitamin and mineral levels checked. Many health problems are a direct result of vitamin and mineral deficiencies.

The three biggest reasons why we push our beach ball underwater:

- Fear
- Unresolved issues or our imprints
- Mind-Body-Spirit disconnection

Things to Consider:
    Believe in yourself, and don't allow anyone or anything to diminish your value and worth. Mind-Body-Spirit are integral, working together as a unit for health and well-being. Develop and write down your personal Mantra, focusing on self-motivation, health and wellness, and passion for a healthier, more inspired life. Consider your relationships with others: Are these people in your life positive and inspiring? Or, negative and "stuck" with their own beach ball issues and challenges. Positive and inspiring relationships and maintaining a "Life Team" are critical assets for a healthy life in the second half of life.
    Do you perform meditation or prayer daily? Do you read positive how-to or "health and lifestyle" books and materials? Practice self-reflection, spend regular time in nature and create a space for solitude and quiet. Are you making positive contributions to your community and world?

Notes and Affirmations:

_____
_____
_____
_____
_____
_____
_____
_____
_____
_____
_____
_____

Deanna's Points to Ponder

What is it in you that is stirring an awakening? For me, this chapter has stirred-up an old saying: "Eat your own dog food" which means, buy your own product, walk your talk. Max has inspired me. I want to transform to achieve being in the best shape of my life, the best version of me I can be. Notice I didn't say "I *need* to get into the best shape of my life". Although I do *need* to according to my doctor, I don't *have* to! We have a choice. We *get* to do _____. I have recently learned, that when we turn a "need" into a "want", powerful results are inevitable. Of course, *our* "wants" must align with God's "wants" for us.

It starts with believing in yourself, really accepting you are worthy. You have to make a conscious decision and an on-purpose plan to be healthy, focusing on envisioning yourself as the best version of you, physically, emotionally, and spiritually. Adapting to new methodologies result in an energy boost, which, in turn, translates to fuel, which is required to get us through the frustration and inevitable pain of change. By embracing these new thoughts and actions, your confidence will go up. Building confidence by being healthy in Mind-Body-Spirt transcends positivity for any of life's transitions you are facing, especially in the area of the job search. I'm excited, inspired, and greatly challenged. I hope you are as well.

Points to Ponder:

- God loves you too much to live a consequence-free life
- Stop being afraid to fail. Failure is part of the process. You'll be 58 years old and still be making mistakes: "Miss Columbia" - *Steve Harvey*
- Too much learning and not enough doing will turn you into an over-motivated underachiever
- You can live with pain a whole lot easier than to live life purposelessly. Passion from pain....you CANNOT BUY THAT!
  - *Beth Moore*

- Your life is either a warning to others or an example to others - *Tony Robbins*
- If you have more withdrawals than deposits in people, then you are emotionally bankrupt - *Bishop T.D. Jakes*
- Making a big change is pretty scary. But, know what is even scarier? Regret - *Zig Ziglar*

CHAPTER NINE

Midlife Crisis
Loss of Real Identity

Just because a man buys a new Porsche Carrera at age sixty-five, does that mean he's experiencing a midlife crisis? Or, because the sixty-year-old woman decides to get plastic surgery, is she experiencing a midlife crisis? **"Midlife Crisis"** is a term coined by Elliott Jacques, referring to a critical phase in human development during the forties to early sixties, based on the character of change points or periods of transition. Whether or not a midlife crisis is a perceived experience or real condition, still has not been determined.

For many, aging into midlife and senior years can be the most difficult stages of life, from physical, mental, and psychological perspectives. Introspective and self-reflection may create a strong desire for change. The transition of identity and self-confidence may be smooth for some but challenging for others. In my midlife journey, I have not experienced crisis due to aging. However, my challenges were driven by life transitions. Crisis and transitions are not mutually exclusive to each other; one may directly drive or impact the other.

People can reach a point in life when they start questioning their life's meaning and purpose. "Is that all there is"? They've lived and done all the things that society said was the blueprint for life's success: Career, family, religion, community etc. The culmination of personal, career or sexual dissatisfactions can lead to *loss of real identity.* Emotional chaos, like a clock's pendulum constantly swinging or moving left to right, right to left nonstop. Until the clock's pendulum stops, in those moments of still, we ponder "what is going on? What has happened to my life? What happened to me!".

The questions that haunted me for years were: "Who's life am I living?" and "What is my true calling?" I use the word "haunted" because I knew my life was not going in the direction I wanted it to go, but I wasn't doing anything to change it. This is the *loss of real identity*, creating and accepting a veneer version of myself to present to the world. While the authentic self peers through, longing to be set free. An internal battle between authentic and fake rages on. In my own life, this battle between the real and faux me, helped create hopelessness, despair, anxiety, anger, and depression. Oftentimes, our mind can blur the difference between the two. Sound familiar?

Crisis in the Chinese culture is both the symbols of danger and opportunity. It can also be your wake-up call to break the barriers holding and keeping you from living your authentic self and true calling. Humans have a need for stimulation, whether it be physical, emotional, or psychological. To feel alive, or as I say COMPLETELY ALIVE, I will go more into this idea in subsequent chapters.

External stimulus - how we look, our face and body, clothing, jewelry, cars, houses, travel and image driven by emptiness - can never fill what's missing inside. One of the best resolutions for midlife crisis and transition, is to know what really makes us happy, fulfilled and complete...AND THEN, GO DO IT! Live authentically!

The midlife passage is an opportunity to "Start Over" fresh, with a new canvas and vivid imagination, painted with experienced hands and mental clarity: Living part-time in the country of Costa Rica, southern Caribbean region. There's a daily stream of new tourists, visiting from around the world.

I can always tell when they've newly arrived because of how they are dressed, especially the women: Females of all adult ages wear obvious make-up cosmetics for their face. Then, I may see them a few days later, and they've ditched the mannequin image for no (or very little) make-up, more relaxed dress, and looking comfortable. When we accept life's natural changes and embrace our authenticity, we can have peace within, the outside image will be what it is, relaxed and real.

I purchased a new Porsche when I was forty-three years old. After owning a Volvo, I was newly single and wanted a hot car. And, the fact was I had always admired the Porsche product and I was finally in a financial position to afford one. So, I purchased one on a lease agreement.

The point is, sometimes people buy things in midlife because they want - and can now afford - them. No crisis, but maybe a "bucket list" thing. Whatever the reason, if they enjoy the purchase and are not harming anyone, then who's to judge. Back to the sixty-year-old woman who decides to get face and neck enhancement surgery. For our example here, she can afford it and wants to improve her visual appeal for herself (and maybe others as well). What's the problem?

In both situations, there's only crisis when it's done to the extreme, bringing harm to themselves or others. Many decisions in midlife are made based upon realization of mortality, discontentment, past and present turmoil, experiences and setbacks. Just make sure you are making the decision for the right reason.

Making career or job changes in midlife versus in earlier stages of life can also create crisis or discontentment. I certainly can relate to this assertion because I've been there, done that, "got the T-shirt, and parting gifts"! STUCK in midlife SUCKS because this is when your personal growth is stalled or completely stops.

Confusion and Despair

Lack (or the absence) of clarity can result in confusion. Midlife is the end of youth. There's no other way to put it. Yes, we can spin it and call "fifty" the new "forty", or "sixty" the new "fifty", but unless the Roman calendar of 365 days per year is somehow changed or altered, 40, 50, 60, 70, 80 and beyond are defined years and decades of chronological life. It is what it is! It's how we **perceive, cope, and manage** the process that counts and matters most. There can be a loss of identities: Who am I now at 50, 60, 70, 80 and so on? Every decade, or age transition period, has one consistent component: Change – be it physical, emotional, psychological, spiritual and/or religious (or all of the above).

Understanding and accepting change are the keys to positive and smooth transition from one stage of life to the next; however, we do not have to give in or give up. Perceived loss of control can bring on confusion, isolation, or even depression. The biological aging process is going to happen no matter what we do, but we can slow it down or manage it *if we want to*. That's the question then: Do we want to? I have talked with people from age 40 to 80, who do not want to do either one - they eat whatever they want, drink alcohol in excess, and intake tobacco on a daily basis, and never exercise. The "I'm going to die anyway." refrain is their mantra, so what the hell?! Until a health crisis arises; then, just maybe, they'll consider making qualitative and measurable changes...if they survive the crisis.

I certainly do not judge or criticize people who make the decision to give up or give in to aging; however, there are positive alternatives. As one man said on a reality TV show "I'm old, fat, and happy, and I'll die that way." It's a matter of personal choice but KNOW it doesn't have to be that way. Do you have total clarity about your health and wellness choices? Or, are you confused? Are you in midlife with crisis and confusion or with clarity and completion? Ask yourself these two very important questions to determine those answers:

1. Is my behavior causing myself, or anyone else, challenges, problems, or harm? If so, seek professional counseling and/or therapy.
2. Can I, or do I, want to make my life count? If you really want to know, read on and get ready to give it some serious thought.

Loss of Productivity and Relevance

Loss of Productivity: Making a positive contribution to society is, for most people, a very important aspect of life. Working and maintaining our independence is also vitally important. Getting older can diminish, or slow down, productivity. Loss of employment without immediate job opportunity, may cause dignity and self-worth to suffer, resulting in more negative financial shift and instability. Entering my 50's, I had a deep sense of dissatisfaction with career, personal accomplishments, and relationships. Why? Because I was not living an authentic life, doing what I wanted to do, achieving personal dreams and visions. This impacted my productivity greatly.

My passion reservoir was depleted and virtually empty. Bouts of depression, excessive alcohol and tobacco use, and confusion became my crutch and sanctuary. Maybe you have experienced the same transitions and behaviors, where something has to give - or maybe you just didn't know what to do. "Stuck Sucks."

As time went on and I gave myself permission to face my beach ball midlife challenges head on, things started to change. I woke up and made a decision to take my life back from a career I didn't want, and move on from negative and stagnating people. I set forth on a path to reinvent myself, get a new vision with fresh dreams, and refill my passion reservoir. If I can do it, so can you - you're not alone *and* you're not a victim.

Many people place their life's value and worth on their work, making a living and providing for their family. Then, when that ability is taken away (or limited), they may feel lost or worthless. I learned from Deanna the importance of maintaining a full and balanced "Grace Tank." It is my hope we all know our total value and balance that value, accordingly without neglecting or negatively impacting other important aspects of our life. We should be productive and passionate about our total life, not just work and what it produces. Loss of productivity can also result in loss of relevance.

Loss of Relevance: In my travels and daily interactions with people from around the world, from their 20's to 80's and beyond, creating and maintaining relevance is critical for integral health and wellness. I learn from listening to people with both my ears and my heart, one to one interaction with a stranger or people we know, can uplift ones spirit. Giving of one's time, can have special meaning, we don't know what our fellow man or woman may be feeling, or living through.

I had a conversation recently with a lady who had just opened a restaurant, here in Costa Rica. I don't know her age, but it's safe to say she is 60-plus, full of life, and passionate about her restaurant business. She asked if I was interested in participating in a group focused on consciousness and healing. Of course, I accepted. Followed by the discussion of the premise and description of this book, I mentioned the challenge of isolation and socialization for many of our fellow Midlifers, Boomers and Seniors. Her response was immediate and passionate: "Just when I have something meaningful to say, the world shuts me out! When I'm around younger people, they act as if I'm not there" She had the courage to say what so many people feel and think, "I no longer matter. I have so much to offer and give, but the world ignores me."

I experienced the same perceptions and experiences in my early to mid 50's. Then, I realized several group and individual dynamics were at play; *I* was the problem, not the world or the people I perceived were casting me aside and ignoring me. This was stunning. I now realize that people, no matter their age, need to relate and connect.

So, I began to proactively engage conversation first, instead of waiting for the opposite. Oftentimes, younger people may be intimidated by our maturity, presence, and experience; then, they use defense mechanisms and pretend not to be interested, or ignore your presence. However, when you meet them where they are in life, and ask about them, instead of talking about you, very positive interactions can occur.

For example, your introduction to connect with others may be something like, "How's your day"? followed by, "What are you working on (or doing)?", "Your interests, or passions?" When we show *genuine* interest in others, without an agenda, you may be surprised how people may drop their guard and open up to the interaction. I have found when young people sense you will listen without judgment and then relate from your perspective, they will feel honored to converse with you.

Two contemporary examples of famous seniors who connect and appeal to millions of Millennials, as well as people of all ages: As of this writing, a 75-year-old politician and 95-year-old actress. Why do they have such appeal with Millennials and people of all ages? They both have the unique appeal for being authentic and real, with sense of humor, passion, campy self-deflection; sometimes, they can be a bit naughty and even radical - serious yet fun with youthful exuberance.

But, I think the most compelling reason is their ability to be relatable, the ability to go to where he, she, and they are in their lives, and to really care. This is the key to connecting and relating to anyone of any age. When we take the "I", "me", and "my" out of the conversation, and focus on "you", "your", and "us", pure magic can happen! A connection where personal relevance and confidence can be elevated. Such a great feeling!

"Everyone needs a passion, that's what keeps life interesting, if you live without passion, you can go through life without leaving any footprints."
- Betty White

I have developed a "Tribe" connection of people from around the world. Not via the internet, but in person during travels and everyday activities. How did I do that? Very simply, by not being afraid to engage and open my mind and heart to others. Our positive, or negative energies, carry a vibration frequency, that resonates even before we open our mouths. These energies either invite or repel others to connect or move on.

The most toxic of connection appeal is that of selfish intent for gain, without giving. When people sense that it's all about you, it's a turn off. But, when it's about them *with* us, then there's a genuine connection, which becomes so vitally important as we age. The exchange of positive energy, ideas and sense of caring is within your and our power no matter our age. These interactions or encounters may be for a few moments or something more lasting, but the point is to have them on a regular basis. They elevate our esteem, relevance, confidence, and they expand our worldview. Passion wins every time! Productivity in giving of one's self not just for monetary gain, but also from the heart, for connection and inner joy.

Relevance starts with knowing that you are important to yourself and others. Do you matter in this world? Physical changes in my life were directly correlated with loss of relevance and self esteem; however, many other contributors play a role in loss of relevance and result in possible isolation: Fear and Insecurity, Lack of Self-Esteem, and Reduced Self-Confidence.

Fear and Insecurity: Change and living in, coping with, and navigating a world dramatically different from the world of a generation ago. Self-doubt (and/or lacking certainty) creeps in.

Lack of Self-Esteem: Loss or lack of self respect, confidence in one's own abilities and assertiveness, can lead to feelings of insecurity and isolation - the "I no longer matter, so I'll hide in my own world." mode.

Reduced Self-Confidence: Loss of belief in one's abilities and faith in one's self - the "I can't", "I don't know how", or "why should I?" mantra.

Potential Signs of Midlife Crisis:

Looking back, do you have a sense of failure or feeling like you haven't accomplished your goals and dreams (or enough in general)? This sense of failure or feeling of lack leads to boredom and loss of interest in life activities, depression, and emotional disturbances, increase in alcohol consumption, increase in tobacco consumption, dramatic change in appearance, angry and disillusioned, impulsive decisions, fear and worry.

We are emotional beings with both positive and negative feelings, thoughts, and behaviors. However, there are situations in our midlife and senior years, when we can experience those (scary) transitions that create negative feelings, thoughts and behaviors. They include, but are not limited to:

- Divorce
- Retirement
- Empty Nest
- Relationship Loss
- Loss of Relevance
- Health Challenges
- Career Transition and Change
- Loss of Income or Financial Well being

Emotional events and situations that most impacted my life:

Births of Sons and Granddaughters

A. Marriage
B. Divorce
C. Death of Family and Friends
D. Layoff/Firing
E. Health Diagnosis
F. Winning My First Big Sale
G. Sons Getting Married
H. Introducing My Sons to Central America
I. Finding My Purpose
J. Forgiveness
K. Moving to Costa Rica
L. Redefining Success

Notice some of the above are negative, and some are positive. Either way, they still impacted me significantly and emotionally.

So, what is emotional and mental good health?

☺ Active, loves to laugh and have fun
☺ Confidence and high self-esteem

- ☺ Doesn't take on a victim's mentality
- ☺ Vitality and passion for living
- ☺ Positive outlook and worldview
- ☺ Balanced lifestyle of work and personal
- ☺ Maintains and cultivates positive relationships
- ☺ Sense of humor; doesn't take life too seriously
- ☺ Adaptable to change, curious, and imaginative
- ☺ Focus on purpose, meaning, legacy, and giving to others

What I Learned:

Deanna taught me to maintain a full "grace tank", filled with passions and dreams, with grace within and for others. Give compassion and express empathy to others because sometimes a kind word can uplift a wounded heart and spirit. Socialization and human interaction are vital components for a fulfilling life, having a healthy and supportive "Life Team". Act my value, not my age, and it's a greater number. Meet transitions and challenges head-on with positive perspective, acceptance of life's many changes and transitions.

Get my priorities straight, live a balanced Mind-Body-Spirit life. I monitor my thoughts and emotions and I flush the negative. Then, I move on from negative and uninspiring people, with well wishes. Now, I am relevant and have immense value. You can't be thankful and irrelevant at the same time. Be the best you can be at any age, starting from the inside out. Seek professional help if psychological and/or emotional issues are beyond your control.

Always have a dream(s) and actively work toward achieving it (them). Develop or maintain resilience. You know life's not meant to be perfect and without challenges. Create a new life vision, and redefine success, based on today, now and in the future. Develop a positive outlook and worldview. Know what makes you happy and fulfilled; then, go do it! People and resources will come to you when you decide to move forward. Open the door!

Create a source of authentic productivity and true giving to others because the more we give the more we gain in return. Develop a strong, positive, and active "Life Team", develop personal- and team-driven passions. Give love and love will come to you; love attracts love. Make a decision and commitment to live a purpose and meaning-based life, your calling is waiting to be released!

Things to Consider:
Healthy socialization and connecting with others in life's second half starts with how we think and feel about *ourselves*. Volunteering one's time and services is a meaningful way to both give back and to elevate one's self-esteem and relevance. Using your experience, abilities, and know-how to help and assist others is a productive use of personal capital and resources. Anyone, a child, millennial, or adult, can benefit from your knowledge, wisdom, and giving, and there's no better way to keep your grace tank filled.

Use your vast life's experience and power as a proactive tool to create and generate the relevance and connections you need and desire. Don't wait for others to light your "passion fuse". You are in control and empowered to do it yourself. You will become a magnet for attracting positive people and meaningful interaction. You are not alone; there are millions of us in the country and world.

Start small, with a trip to a coffee shop, where there are always people to engage, listen, and connect. Create your own social group. Book clubs are a special and intellectual forum for creative exchange and debate. More about volunteering in subsequent chapters.

Engage people with an open mind and remember their name. One such way to powerfully engage on a personal level: Take the time to listen to their name and then repeat it. I usually put the person's name in my notes on my cell phone. If and when I see them again, I can call them by name, and they feel special. They may have forgotten yours but that's okay, they will remember it, since you remembered theirs. Show your real self, be an example of authenticity and caring, people will want to connect with you.

There are periods of life when the focus can be more on looking good than feeling good. In the second half of our lives, our focus should be on both looking and feeling good about ourselves, with balanced Mind-Body-Spirit. We should be proud of every wrinkle, gray hair, and change - we earned it! Age change and age perspective start from within. Join our "Over 50" tribe and blog post. We also have listings of numerous cohort and tribe blog and podcast resources located on our website and facebook pages. Connect, engage, live, and learn. Passion wins every time!

Exercise:

What will you do in the next seven days to connect with others?

_____
_____
_____
_____
_____
_____

What most nourishes your inner being and spirit, and why? Examples; nature, quiet time, meditation, human interaction etc...

_____
_____
_____
_____
_____
_____
_____
_____

Deanna's Inspirational Insights

Why do some people think, in their 40's or 50's, there has to be some sort of "midlife crisis"? Just naming it a "crisis" should tell us it is something we would want to repel. Who would volunteer to sign up for a crisis anyway? Oh wait, some of us do. What if you look at this time of your life as an *opportunity* to take stock, rather than a crisis, and see if you are where you want to be? And, if the answer is no, then it is time to evaluate and work on a plan to get you where you want to be. I prefer to call it "midlife review". In this "review", we acknowledge there is a "do-over" button, if we care, and dare, to use it.

When assessing where you are, compared to where you want to be, review the most important milestones first: Faith, relationships, health, finances, career, etc. Never compare yourself to others. In coaching, I often assist people in transitioning to entrepreneurship from traditional employment. In this shift, I remind them to never compare their beginning to someone else's middle. It seems to be our default to compare ourselves or our situation to someone else's "perceived success". How discouraging. Not only discouraging, but it also gets in the way of our plan, and, in the very least, it slows us down. Slowing down is the last thing we need to volunteer to do.

I believe any chapter of your life can be summarized by how well you manage what I call your "grace tank". Our grace tank, ideally, should have a healthy balance, and, at most times, an over-flowing balance filling an outside reservoir as well. But, there are times we will find ourselves overdrawn on our grace tank. Chalk that up to surmise that the enemy has been winning more lately than our advocate. When that happens, it is time to fill the grace tank.

My relationship advice has always been: Out-serve each other *without keeping score*. You can be successful in this only when you have a discipline in place that continuously fills and replenishes your grace tank. We all know people, or have been in positions at work, or in situations, where we experience the life being sucked out of us. If we are not intentional with how we deal with those interactions, we may find ourselves overdrawn in our grace tanks, turning our actions and reactions into "blocking blessings".

Have you ever made a major decision at a time where your grace tank was not at a healthy level? A decision made out of reaction, rather than well thought out and pro-active planning, balanced with seeking and confirming His will? During transitional periods (job loss, empty nesters, divorce, financial shifts, health concerns, or feeling of loss of relevance), I recommend to take a grace tank inventory and confirm you are still at a healthy level.

Here is how you can check your tank: Think of that person (we all have one or two) that you may dearly love, but when you see their caller-ID come up on the phone, you grimace. You check the time, and most, if not all of the time, you let the call go to voicemail. You just do not have the time, stomach, or *grace* to speak with them at the moment. That's when you know you need a refill.

If you do not have a process in which to regularly fill your grace tank, then make one. Some examples of grace tank fillers are: Worship, prayer, Bible study, date-nights, fun activities, fellowship with like-minded people, time with your mentor, meditation, exercise, volunteering, and alone time. Review and reconfirm your 7-8 critical needs from Chapter 6.

Any time you can claim that you are one with your Creator, then there is no room for confusion. Our enemy owns confusion. So, if you find yourself confused and unable to recognize opportunity, or if you feel stuck, please know that is a place where our enemy wants you to stay, to dwell forever - if he can get away with it. However, it is your choice. I pray you realize you are empowered, by the Holy Spirit, to renounce confusion and (re)claim your destiny in His name to reach your full potential, to know you are worthy, to make extremely valuable contributions, current and future.

CHAPTER TEN

Give Yourself Permission
You're in Control

It's hard to dance in life
when you're stuck in
the wrong job or career,
bad relationship, the past,
low self esteem or indecision.

The personal journey to new passion and new life is a decision, one based upon the want - and need - to do so, to change somehow. Just about everything we receive in life that is good is earned and usually comes with a price. If a fulfilling and meaningful life were easy, then everyone would achieve it. In fact, it is not easy. *But*, neither is it impossible. It starts with a decision and commitment to personal growth, to take the steps necessary for change. The biggest challenge of living into our 50's (and well beyond) is self-doubt and being stuck in the past, like the proverbial 2-ton elephant tied to a 2-pound stake who thinks it cannot move because it has been conditioned by its master or trainer to believe so.

Are you in control of your own life and destiny? Remember, there are five reasons why you will not achieve your dreams and passions for a fulfilled life:

- Self-doubt
- Procrastination
- Lack of emotional and/or physical energy and/or health
- Allowing negative words and/or energies from others to "sink your ship"
- Fear of change/stuck in the past

Self-doubt: Who or what made you identify with low esteem and/or confidence in yourself? Until you answer and overcome the why and who of this question, you cannot move forward.

Procrastination: Delaying, postponing and putting off important decisions. *"I'll get around to it later"*. But later never seems to come. Small steps lead to big steps.

Lack of emotional and/or physical energy and/or health: Mind-Body-Spirit disconnect. Physical health starts with good or positive mental health and outlook.

Allowing negative words and/or energies from others to "sink your ship": Positive energy and motivation are connectors for healthy Mind-Body-Spirit. Negative people create and pass on negative energies. Like weeds in a garden, if they remain they will consume the garden. Are you attracting negative instead of positive people and energies into your life, do you know why? You can imagine and create the life that you want, no one else can do it for you.

Fear of change: The reason why you are stuck in the "now" is because you are still stuck in the past. Read that sentence again. Now, answer these questions:

Am I sick and tired of being sick and tired?

- ☐ Yes
- ☐ No

What are my passions? What are people or things that brings you joy, happiness, increases your energy, gets you excited and makes "your engine rev"?

_____
_____
_____
_____
_____
_____

What are my "Stuck" points? You either can't or won't move to action, decision or taking responsibility. Examples; stuck in the wrong job, career or relationship?

_____
_____
_____
_____
_____
_____

Does my life have real meaning? If not, why not?

- ☐ Yes
- ☐ No

_____

Define your "why not":

_____
_____
_____
_____
_____

Am I contributing something good and positive to the world? If not, why not?

☐ Yes
☐ No

Write your "why not":

_____
_____
_____
_____
_____

Do I love me? If not, why not?

☐ Yes
☐ No

Why not?

_____

_____

_____

_____

What are the things in my life causing stress?

_____

_____

_____

_____

_____

What is my legacy to the world and my family?

_____

_____

_____

_____

_____

Do you have people in your life who will support you and be happy with your changes? If not, then consider expanding your network with people who are on a similar life path. This is also an opportunity to get out of your comfort zone and develop fresh, new relationships. One easy way is to join the "Over 50, Starting Over" blog post or facebook page, where people just like you are sharing, connecting, and having fun growing together.

Your journey is about growth, meaning, and fulfillment for you, and you are the Architect, Director, and CEO of your life. You get to own it! So, go deeper into your life, honor and love yourself, heal your body, and have the courage to truthfully answer these hard questions (and any others) about your life. Find the answers that fit YOU best. Give yourself permission to be the best version of you!

Passion needs fuel, and it is based upon your honest ability to generate the positive physical, emotional, and spiritual energies. Join with others on the same path (albeit in their own "lane"), so you can love and support your individual (and group) challenges and goals.

People value what they own. I've never seen anyone wash a rental car or take a rented tuxedo to the cleaners. However, we own our bodies. So, why don't we value them enough to take care of them? TAKE OWNERSHIP OF YOUR SECOND HALF OF LIFE! *You're in control!*

Throughout my life, I've made many decisions and plans. In hindsight, some are great, some good, and some not so good. I constructed plans to support my decisions, and while, not all of my plans were realized, I owned my decisions, whether it was moving to a new city, seeking professional help, or pursuing my passion. The very first step before we can deal with change or our beach ball issues, is to *make the decision* to take action. This is what moves us forward.

Change and Adapt

Wisdom is power. Age, coupled with wisdom, provides us with life's opportunity to put what we've learned and experienced into action. "Over 50", the physical body is not what it was at 20, 30, or even 40; however, with the integral Mind-Body-Spirit balance and conscious focus on health and wellness, we can still live healthy and vibrant lives for many decades past 50.

Today, we have the knowledge, power, and tools for extending our individual life expectancy well beyond that of our parents' generation. Health and wellness are a decision and commitment we make with many options and paths available for living healthy and rewarding lives for however long we may live.

Throughout our lives, many people live through a version of the principle of delayed gratification. Plan, wait, plan, and get. Save, plan, save, and plan. So, they plan, save, deny themselves, and never give themselves permission to get or receive. Deanna taught me the principle of "giving myself permission" to break out of the pack and go for what I want in life. For me, this was a revelation and a turning point. Do you really know what you want in life? And, an equally important question: Do you think you deserve it?

The question of "Over 50" is: "What do I do now?" For so long, I resisted change. I was an angry young man; I knew I had to change, knew I wanted to change, knew I could change, but I resisted. I didn't find my pathway to change until I left my home town and consciously - and willingly - embraced change.

Give Yourself Permission
Reactivate Your Essence

Essence. For our purposes here, essence is the core nature, or most important qualities, of a person or thing. The intrinsic or indispensable quality (or qualities) that serve to characterize or identify something. For example, the essence of democracy is the freedom to choose.

A while back, I thought the best way to determine my personal core essence was to ask others. Thus, here are some examples from the feedback of what people saw (and continue to see) in me: Charismatic, thoughtful, professional, insightful, creative, unique, caring, communicative, spiritual and visionary.

What would people say about your personal essence? Make a list. Then, compare it to the results of your DISC Personality Profile.

_____

_____

_____

_____

_____

People have different views and opinions of each other and themselves. More often than not, people can see things in you that you may not see in yourself or think about. No one knows you better than you do, and no one knows me better than I do. Here's how I characterize my essence in the following core qualities: Insightful, caring, passionate, spiritual, creative, loving, visionary, inspirational, generous and purpose-driven.

From ages nineteen to twenty-six, my essence qualities were organic and filled with passion and energy. Then, when I entered Corporate America and began to focus on money, affluence, and status, all of which created egoism, my essence began to erode. Egoism masks authenticity, real meaning, and love. Now, I can clearly see it in families where the parents are so busy with career and the pursuit of money - they fail to give their children what the children really want and need most: Their parents' love and time.

My 50's made me realize I had lost much of my essence over the years. This can, and often does, happen when we're focused on our emotional energy sacrifices. With more energy (outputs) to others, with little to no focus on inputting and replenishing our own essence reservoir, we may settle into a "stuck" or stagnant state. Don't you think it's time to refocus on your *own* core essence and needs? It's not too late; actually, it's the perfect time. Why? Because you can and *should*.

Having worked in Corporate America for over thirty years, I became intimately aware of corporate "mission statements". I have written several of them for different businesses over the years. However, I'd never written my *personal* "mission statement" until I got serious about taking control of my life's destiny and its priorities.

A mission statement is a declaration of the core purpose and focus of a company, organization, or person and normally remains *unchanged* over time. A mission statement is different from a vision statement in that the former is the cause and the latter is the effect.

A mission is something to be accomplished, whereas a vision is something to be pursued for that said accomplishment. The mission statement is the reason for existing and should guide the actions of the company or person.

This is my personal mission statement:

"Live a balanced life with Mind-Body-Spirit, fully integrated, filled with self-love and love for family and others. Passion and energy driven by vision and legacy for a full and complete life."

The following quote crystallized my focus for my "Over 50" life's mission:

> *"The two most important days in your life are the day you born and the day you find out why."* - Mark Twain

Being a father and grandfather are the most important gifts in my life. They give me the fulfillment as the primary reasons why I was born. In my 50's, I began to understand I was now ready and positioned for other reasons for living. If you're blessed enough to live past your so-called "prime", then you have a calling, whether you realize it or not. What is yours? Don't know, create one.

What I Learned:

- With so much self-love, I am able to put others before myself
- Our essence can be diminished over time, and we are usually unaware it even has happened
- Knowing one's calling is to know your why

Notes and Affirmations:
_____
_____
_____
_____
_____

1. Am I COMPLETELY ALIVE? Or, am I just going through life's motions? Write down why or why not:

_____
_____
_____
_____
_____

Here are a few descriptions that define COMPLETELY ALIVE:

- ☺ Driven by passion
- ☺ Enjoying life to its full
- ☺ Living in the moment
- ☺ Controlling your thoughts and emotions
- ☺ Eager to greet each day with a positive world-view
- ☺ Energetic and filled with passion for life
- ☺ Aware and conscious of your breath and being

Reimagine and Rediscover

Examples of Baby Boomer Dreams and Passions:

Live Abroad	Writer - Author	Travel	Entrepreneur
Financial Security	Artist	Retirement	
Debt Free	Love	Philanthropy	Education
Musician	Dream Home		Boat
Rest and Relaxation	Volunteer	Inventor	Fishing Boat Charter
Dream Car	Executive	Ministry	Outreach Gardening
Health & Fitness	Legacy Adventure	Freedom	Career Change
Fun	Dream Vacation	Coach	Mentor	Purpose
	Meaning	Calling	

Life Team - Your Collaborative Partnership

Socialization is the process by which we learn social skills, among other things. This process is where people become aware of lifestyles and behaviors. Erik Erikson, was a German born American developmental psychologist and psychoanalyst known for his theory on psychosocial social development of human beings. He may be most famous for coining the phrase identity crisis. Erikson's Eight Stages of Psychological Development:

1. Learn basic trust versus mistrust (Hope)
2. Learning autonomy versus shame (Will)
3. Learning initiative versus guilt (Purpose)
4. Industry versus inferiority (Competence)
5. Learning identity versus identity diffusion (Fidelity)
6. Learning intimacy versus isolation (Love)
7. Learning generatively versus self absorption (Care)
8. Integrity versus despair (Wisdom)

Stage 6 *Intimacy versus Isolation covers the period of early adulthood, when people are exploring personal relationships.* Erikson believed it was vital for people to develop committed and close relationships with others. The ability to create and form long and lasting relationships with people is critical.

Since socialization is a process based upon connecting with our fellow human beings, as we age, our loss of socialization can impact many, if not all, eight stages. From youth, it's our classmates, pals, and friends who share our interests. At this age, we share interests in sports, cars, or academics. However, in the parent stage, we typically have a team of others who have children. During the career, or work, stage we typically have colleagues. But, "Over 50", it's a more concerted effort to maintain relationships. These relationships can diminish, and shared interests may change our connection with others. Often, you may have to actively look for a new team and create fresh relationships.

Through all of your life's transitions - divorce, empty nest, relational loss, job loss/shift, loss of relevance, financial shifts, midlife crisis and health issues - your current team may have developed intentionally or through life's circle of chance. Maintaining existing relationships and cultivating new ones are vital to living a connected and fulfilling life. Your Life Team is your core circle (and extended lifeline) of friendly connections. We have different relationships for diverse reasons and needs, all playing their respective and reciprocal roles.

A *team* is a collaborative effort which works together for a common objective, whereas a *"Life Team"* is *your* team, handpicked by *you* to help *you* achieve *your* individual goals and objectives.

My Life Team Consists of the Following:

Professional:
- Pastor or Spiritual Advisor
- Attorney
- CPA (Certified Public Accountant), Financial Planner
- Life and Career Coach
- Psychologist
- Physician
- Mentor
- Subject Matter Experts (SME)

Personal:
- Family
- Friends
- Advisors
- Confidants

A Life Team fills the individual need for Mind-Body-Spirit health and direction. A key attribute for both professional and personal contribution is positive intent and action. All too often, we have people on our Life Team who are not the right fit for us or our personalities, goals, and objectives.

Another important aspect of a Life Team member is honesty - these people will tell you the truth as they see it, not what they think you want to hear, and they bring only positive value to your team. It's crucial to speak with at least one person on your Life Team daily for sync and connection. We also connect via text and email, however there's no substitute for in person over coffee, on the phone, etc.

Over the decades, my Life Team has expanded, and contracted, then expanded again. There is no set or recommended number of members for a Life Team, it's all based on one's individual needs.

During my corporate working days, there were people within my life team who played such huge supportive and spiritual roles. Sometimes, we all just need someone to say, "Hang in there."-"Stay strong.", "You can do it.", "God is on your side.", "It's all temporary.", "I got your back.", etc.

In the past, my team has expanded to include more than fifty people from all over the world, plus my Los Angeles, Houston, Atlanta, and North Carolina teams. Gradually, and in the last 10 years or so, more and more young people, ranging in age from 24 to 40s, have joined my Life Team. It is so rewarding to share perspectives and value with people of *all ages*, and it enriches my worldview, and expands options, and enhances choices - a cross-pollination of ideas, opinions, and experiences. Priceless!

What I Learned:

Can people change? Yes, by choice, or having no alternative but to do so. Change before you have to - *don't wait for a life-changing event or illness.* Try new things, like: Yoga, Pilates, Tai Chi - in a group setting, each of these facilitates socialization, meditation, and interaction. Replace, change, or augment your comfort zone. Get comfortable with being a little *UN*comfortable. I've learned to be uncomfortable in order to increase motivation and take action. Learning and experiencing new and different things is always uncomfortable...at first.

Be proactive with health matters. Focus on mobility and movement.

Things to Consider:

Please answer the following questions:

Are you physically able to engage in 30 minutes of exercise or movement to elevate heart rate daily? If not, what can you do to get to that point? (Check with your healthcare provider for guidance)
❏ Yes
❏ No

Do you drink at least 8 glasses of water daily?
❏ Yes
❏ No

What does your daily diet consist of?
_____
_____
_____
_____
_____

Do you eat fresh fruits and vegetables?
❏ Yes
❏ No

Do you drink alcohol? If so, how much daily?
❏ Yes
❏ No
_____

Do you use tobacco, cigarettes, cigars, or pipe? If so, how much daily?
❏ Yes
❏ No

What health problems do you have?
_____
_____
_____

How many medications do you take daily? (Check with your healthcare provider on ways to reduce the number, dosage, etc.)
_____
_____
_____
_____

Do you have a Life Team?
- ❏ Yes
- ❏ No

If you don't have a Life Team, brainstorm. Who is *a best fit* to recruit? Do you know your personality type? Read Deanna's DISC personality types at the end of this chapter.

People say the glass is half-full or half-empty, and then there's a cliché, "Fifty is the new 40". I'm concerned more with *owning the glass* than whether or not it's half-full or half-empty. If I own the glass, then I control what's in it. Fifty is 50 - we are who we are and know what we know. Personally, I have no interest in being 30 again - been there done that. Be the best you can be now, no matter what the age.

At almost 60, here are my "Top 20 Positives" that I did not fully understand, experience, or practice at ages 30, or 40, even 50:

1. I'm only concerned with the things in life I *can* control, and I don't worry about the ones I *can't*. Empathy, concern, and support are all important; *however, worry is not an option*

2. Thankful and filled with gratitude every day
3. Assertive - I enjoy saying no (in a kind but heart-healthy way)
4. Non-judgmental
5. Practice forgiveness
6. Golden Rule – Treat people the way I want to be treated
7. Self-love and letting go
8. More selective when connecting with people
9. I stopped explaining my thoughts and actions for validation
10. Comfortable in my own skin
11. Able to express love to others without expecting any in return
12. Focus on Mind-Body-Spirit health
13. Materialism does not matter
14. Debt-free and financially comfortable
15. Focused on others as much as myself
16. Keep the passion fire burning and always have a dream
17. Simplicity
18. Adaptability
19. Positive thinking and purpose-driven
20. Passion-driven

Exercise:
What are your "Top 20 Positives" in your life right now? Write them down. They should be similar to your mantra, if they are not similar then rethink your list. Don't worry about filling all spaces. If you have less than 20, that's okay - it's your life, additional space is also provided at the end of this chapter.

_____
_____
_____
_____
_____
_____
_____
_____

_____

_____

_____

_____

_____

_____

_____

Focusing on *being*, instead of *becoming*, is so liberating. Having nothing to prove to anyone is the ultimate freedom. So many older people take the same insecurities from their 30's and 40's into their 50's and beyond, holding onto an illusion of the past or what was, only to experience anxiety when old insecurities no longer get the same response, result, or expectation. Literally, it's time to grow up.

The BIGGEST beach ball question that changed my life, and may change yours:
"If you could be given just one desire for only YOU by God, or life what would it be?"

"We are not meant to be perfect, but we are meant to try! No matter our age, never ever stop trying to live a bigger life. Start over."
- Max Gilreath

Notes and Affirmations:

_____
_____
_____
_____
_____
_____
_____
_____
_____
_____

DISC Personality Profile Assessments

The decision-making process is different for each of us. This is why I believe it is important to know your personality type because as you go through any decision-making process - how you attack decisions and how successful you are at making the right one - is based on your personality type. I use the DISC Assessment.

According to discprofile.com: DiSC® is a personal assessment tool used to improve work productivity, teamwork, leadership, and communication.

DISC measures your personality and behavioral style. It does not measure intelligence, aptitude, mental health, or values. DISC profiles describe human behavior in various situations, for example, how you respond to challenges, how you influence others, your preferred pace and how you respond to rules and procedures.

Here is a high-level overview of each personality: Keep in mind, we are all a combination of some (or all) of these, resulting in 25 subtitled personality types.

D - Dominance   Drivers. These are your natural born leaders, exceptional decision-makers, your Eagle Scouts, entrepreneurs, Admirals, CEOs, etc. Their strengths: Takes charge, likes power and authority, confident, very direct, adventurous, bold, determined, competitive, and self-reliant. Weaknesses: Can hurt others' feelings, can turn people off, overlooks details. I often use examples such as Donald Trump, or anyone on the panel from the show, "Shark Tank". Compared to an animal or bird, the **D** Personality would be a lion or an eagle and represents approximately 3% of the population whose results are high in this category. Their tagline: "Let's do it now!". My tagline for "D" is "Ready, fire, aim!"

I - Influence   Expressive. These are folks who have never met a stranger, very outgoing. Their strengths: Good conversationalist, outgoing, entertains others, fun-loving, impulsive, enjoys change, creative, energetic, optimistic, promoter. Weaknesses: Can waste time, won't be quiet and listen, loses sight of the task. Lucille Ball always comes to mind when thinking of an extreme **I** Personality. Compared to an animal or bird, the **I**

Personality would be an otter or a peacock, and 11% of the general population are high in this category. Their tagline: "Trust me! It'll work out!". My tagline for an "I" Personality is "A party waiting for a place to happen."

S - Steadiness   These people are the hard workers we can always count on. Their strengths: Steady, loyal, good listeners, calm, enjoys routine, sympathetic, patient, understanding, reliable, avoids conflict. Weaknesses: Can be slow to act, maintains a low profile, may seem unrealistic. I relate this personality to a great receptionist, or administrative assistant, relationship sales, or any "behind-the-scenes" person. Compared to a bird or animal, the **S** personality would be a dove or Golden Retriever and represent 69% of the people who score high in the **S** category. Their tagline: "Let's keep things the way they are!". My tagline for "S" Personalities: "Someone has to stay behind and get all of the work done!", and my coaching advice for them is to recite this phrase to others as much as is necessary: "Don't mistake my kindness as a weakness!"

C - Compliance   Well-organized. They prefer to work alone, so their exactness can be re-verified. You will want a **C** Personality as your CPA. Their strengths: Loves detail, very logical, diplomatic, factual, deliberate, controlled, inquisitive, predictable. Weaknesses: Can appear rigid, resistant to change, too serious. Compared to a bird or animal, the **C** Personality would be an owl or beaver. Only 17% of the population scores high in the **C** Category. Their tagline: "How was it done in the past?". My tagline for "C" Personalities: "Pray with your legs. Keep moving forward". My coaching advice is always: "Let's get you out of your 'permanent beta' mindset". **C**s tend to always want to take one more class, or change one more thing on their résumé or research just a little bit more. A shout-out to our editor, Robin Sweet: I'm so thankful to God that He made you with an extra dash of **C**; it is why you are so good at what you do!

You can probably observe how each of these personality types would go about tackling life's tough decisions. Some with ease while others are paralyzed in non-commitment ("paralysis by analysis") to move forward with a decision of any kind. I encourage you to take a DISC Personality Profile Assessment if you do not know your personality type. It is so insightful as to how you deal with other personalities as well as how to understand your strengths and weaknesses. In case you are interested, Max's personality is a **D-I** with a subtitle of "Director". I am a **S-I** with a subtitle of "Advisor".

CHAPTER ELEVEN

*Completely Alive
Endless Possibilities*

How did we lose our passion for life? How do we regain it, and, moreover, keep it? Change is a process, not necessarily a destination, and the bigger the change, the more challenging the journey may be. I've learned to be patient yet persistent once I've made a decision to change and transition towards transformation.

Major life change can be frustrating, especially when we're seeking a quick fix or immediate resolution to life transitions and imprints. The first questions I now ask when facing difficult transitional change is, "How did I get here? How should I approach the situation? And, what is the desired outcome?" On many levels, becoming an author and writing this book have been the most difficult yet rewarding vocational endeavors of my life.

There were two transitions that I avoided, even dreaded, writing about (much less reading my own words) because of deep emotional pain, which created anxiety to the point of weeping all over again: Divorce and relational loss of my brother, Chip. No other transition - job loss or career transition, empty nest, financial shifts, health issues, midlife crisis or loss of relevance - has had the emotional and psychological impacts as divorce or relational loss.

The third unresolved issue were imprints from my childhood, as they related to my parents and the pain of feeling alone and unloved. Forgiveness of myself and others has helped ease this issue. Do you have unresolved past life transitions and imprints, preventing you from moving forward? We cannot be **completely alive** with passion and fulfillment, with unresolved beach ball transitions and issues.

For example, at age 57, I thought I had forgiven myself and others involved; however, the depth of the pain and hurt endured, settled into a deep subconscious level, lying dormant in my heart and being. The transitions of divorce and relational loss of my brother Chip were still there, along with parental hurt and pain; these were ghosts of the past, haunting my very being. Just when I thought they were resolved, like the submerged beach ball, I could only hold them under for so long before they surged back to the top. I had not totally let go, so the next surge was inevitably coming. Maybe you can relate to past hurt and pain that you still carry with you?

I had come a long way since my last job, growing in confidence that my transition to a new and bigger life was happening, even if it felt like it was taking longer than I thought it should. I felt as though I was in middle passage of a long journey, having made so much progress towards transformation, yet I still had distance to cover. Travel for me has a way of clearing mental fog, providing physical and emotional rejuvenation and clarity. My inner voice said, "You need to travel and get away from your daily environment and routine".

I followed that inner voice and made plans to sequentially visit Panama, Nicaragua, and Costa Rica, all located in Central America. Since I had visited Panama previously and knew Costa Rica intimately, I needed a new destination for inspiration and perspective - I chose Nicaragua. I have occasion to awake at 4:00AM in the morning, an emotional "wake-up call". This happens for one of two reasons: 1.) The need to write down what is in my spirit and consciousness, and/or 2.) The need to take action, or deeply consider, a decision. It was at 4:00AM when I made the decision for this travel journey, knowing it would hold special meaning for my life. In life's second half, I pay particular attention to these "messages" because I believe they are from God or one of my guardian angels. Little did I know the life-changing transformations that lay ahead, my heart and mind were open to adventure, filled with expectation and possibilities to learn and explore.

First destination Panama. A friend recommended a small island named Bastimentos on the Isla Bastimentos, which is a small but beautiful, quaint Third World island with no cars and one sidewalk. After a ten minute boat ride from the Islands of Bocas Del Toro "mouths of the bull" archipelago. This province is a "biological fantasy" blessed by nature, with unparalleled tropical beauty. Beautiful green jungle hues, white sand beaches and deep blue to blue-green surf's of the Caribbean Ocean. Indigenous Western Caribe. Latino, Indian, African, and multicultural people.

It was my first day on the island, after dinner I went to bed early, tired from the journey. The next morning I wasn't happy with my first night at the lodge. The paper-thin mattress and pillow made for an uncomfortable night's rest, so I ventured out to find a more accommodating lodge or hotel on the water…and I found it.

From the moment I stepped onto the property, the energy was positive and very appealing, with only six rooms and a separate room directly over the water. I met the owner, Chris, who is a German expat. Chris, with his wife, had purchased the lodge. He was such a friendly and sincere person. I asked him if he could recommend a Yogi (Yoga) for a practice session, he said the local Yogi's name is Heather.

I had not practiced in a few weeks and needed to re-engage in my routine. As fate would have it, the Yogi's husband was repairing the deck, and the owner introduced me, he facilitated the introduction to his wife, to schedule a private session. Meanwhile, I asked Chris if he had an available room. He stated the "VIP room" ☺ over the water with the hammock in front was $40 per night and would be available in a few days. I immediately booked the room and felt assured this is where I was supposed to be.

When the time came, I moved into my new digs. It had a hammock and rocking chair on the porch, and the room itself had hardwood flooring and large cut outs for windows, with an extraordinary view of the bay. The restaurant and deck were over the water with hammocks for lodge guests and restaurant patrons to relax and comfortably enjoy the splendid view or watch as people boarded and debarked from the local boat dock right next door. Engulfed by the biodiversity, it was the deep blue and coral-blue surf that captivated my focus. I began to be more and more aware of, and drawn to the surrounding waters. Heather would explain my attraction to the color blue, later in this chapter.

Everything I needed was in the room, including a small table that I could keep my fresh fruit and vegetables on, so I could make my daily smoothies. (Yes, I travel with my own smoothie blender. Don't you?) ☺ Two resident sweetheart dogs and a big, white, fluffy rabbit named Bonita would come into my room at night and sleep beside and under my bed. I awoke each morning to a rooster crowing and a variety of birds singing in the trees next door, and, combined with the constant white noise of the surf, this was simple BLISS! Out of the city and societal box of Urban America.

When I met Heather, the Yogi, I was immediately drawn to her calm spirit and peaceful energy. She came to the lodge for a personal Vinyasa Yoga session for two other guests and me. This was my first time experience with Vinyasa Yoga since I normally practice Hot Yoga.

The word "Vinyasa" can be translated as "arranging something in a special way," like yoga poses for example. In Vinyasa yoga classes, students coordinate movement with breath to flow from one pose to the next. Ashtanga, Baptiste Yoga, Jivamukti, Power Yoga, and Prana Flow could all be considered forms of Vinyasa Yoga. Vinyasa is also the term used to describe a specific sequence of poses (Chaturanga to Upward-Facing Dog to Downward-Facing Dog) commonly used throughout a Vinyasa class.

At the end of the one-hour session, she cradled each of our heads in her hands as a final meditation. This lasted only ten to 15 seconds; however, I felt the energy and warmth from her hands, and it was relaxing and comforting. Then, she spoke of chakra balancing and alignment, which she could perform for each of us by appointment only.

According to Eastern traditions and thought, there are seven chakras in the human body, and they are the centers in the body in which energy constantly flows through.

First Chakra – Red – Root Chakra, most dense Chakra "fight or flight" response
Second Chakra – Orange – Below the navel, positive nurturing of ourselves
Third Chakra – Yellow – Solar Plexus, vibrant, optimistic, and full of energy
Fourth Chakra – Green – Heart, love and transformation
Fifth Chakra – Blue (sapphire blue or turquoise) – Throat, connects with the Divine and it is the color that we associate with Heaven
Sixth Chakra – Indigo – Third eye, opens the door to the Divine
Seventh Chakra – Violet – Crown, offers an inner sense of wholeness

Chakra balance and alignment are processes and adjustments for peak energy performance. I scheduled a chakra balance and alignment with

Heather for a Saturday morning at the lodge, the perfect environment for meditation and calm introspection. Over the next few days, I thought intently about the people I met over a three-week period between Costa Rica and Panama, and all the signs, events, and affirmations along the way.

It had been many years since I experienced a balance between energy input and output, for trusting others. For example, I had very little motivation to engage strangers for conversation and interaction. However, my intentions for engaging others was sincere and unfiltered. To receive unfiltered responses in kind, created positive-energy exchange. The law of attraction was intentional, free-flowing, clear, and effortless.

My physical energy level was increasing by the day. I started with a fresh fruit smoothie at 7:00AM, followed by a six to 8 mile walk and jog, yoga on a few mornings; then, I usually had lunch, including a fresh, green vegetable smoothie. In the afternoon and evenings, I wrote and explored. My body and mind were in total harmony; however, my inner spirit was uneasy, and I understood why.

While forgiveness, time, and reconciliation had healed many wounds, I was not fully liberated from past transitions and childhood. The emotional drain on my spirit created an exhausting physical experience. I felt as though I had run 20 miles of a 26-mile marathon. My body felt heavy and burdened, and I didn't want this feeling in my life any longer. I sensed something profoundly miraculous was about to happen...and it did!

Random Guidance is Freedom's Path

When Heather arrived at the lodge at 10:00AM for the chakra balance and alignment, she lit white sage incense and the morning Om mantra of a chant played in the background. I laid on my back on the bed in Savasana, or resting, position. Heather covered my eyes with her hands, and within six or 8 minutes, I was in a trance-like state, going deeper into total meditative conscience. I was aware of Heather's presence and could sense her hand moving from one chakra or energy point to another. During my journey, I had visions like a movie reel of people, times, and events: As a small boy, my parents, relatives, my children as small boys, and even my ex-wife. All of the people in this "film" were happy, except for me as a child. I was standing with a sad and blank facial expression, feeling alone and unhappy.

Even though Heather was silent during this process, I sensed she spent more time in the solar plexus or liver area than the other chakra zones. I felt her hand make a motion as if to pull or remove energies from the different chakra areas. I estimated I was "under" for approximately thirty to 40 minutes.

I heard Heather call my name, slowly bringing me back to full consciousness. When I opened my eyes, I was totally incoherent and fatigued. It took several minutes for me to fully comprehend my surroundings. I have experienced deep meditative states with Om and Yoga practice before, but none could compare to this.

Heather asked if I was okay and if I had anything to share with her. I responded I needed more time for full awareness and recovery because I was totally drained! Then, she said, "I have a few things to share with you." So, she revealed the following:

- "You had some old and negative energy stored up from your childhood in the liver area, or solar plexus."
- She communicated specific details of traumatic experiences from my childhood related to my father and detailed scenarios of my divorce
- She said my primary chakra color at the beginning of the session was yellow/gold in the solar plexus area (the liver), and by the end of the session, my primary chakra color was light blue for the throat area. This is especially profound since public speaking and oratory are a big part of my essence
- She said she had removed the negative, old energies which were blocking my unrestricted energy flow throughout my body. This blockage explained why I had anxiety
- She said God has planned such a meaningful and bright future for me, it would be difficult for me to comprehend

At that point, I completely broke down and wept to the point of hyperventilating. Ironically, I had not wept with such purging emotion since the aftermath of my divorce during that church service years ago. I immediately thought of the doctor's affirmation more than fifty years ago. This is my time - time to know, time to understand, and time to accept my calling and purpose. This was the most impactful, therapeutic event I have ever experienced. I shared with Heather that affirmation - I guess it could be called a prediction - from Chapter 2 ("Something Special") from my pediatrician. I now understood how I've been guided, and even protected, throughout my life in preparation for how I can now be of service and a guiding light for people in the second half of life.

At the end of the session, I felt like a huge weight had been lifted from my chest and shoulders. I no longer carried the burden of past pain, hurt, and sorrow. I was now truly free! I needed one last cry, to release and uproot the past and to be set free. Maybe you need to have one last cry, to free and remove deep-rooted past pain and hurt as well.

For the entire day after the chakra balance and alignment, I had a deepened sense of gratitude, forgiveness, and joy in my life with a peace-filled heart and spirit. Everything (the good, the bad, and the ugly), all the experiences of my life had led me to be the man I am today. I am forgiving myself for my unintentional mistakes and failings in life and letting go of the past. I am forgiving others for their harms (whether intentional or not) against me, as well as their unintentional mistakes to me. Yes, they are all forgiven, because no human being is perfect. Sometimes, it takes the insight, talent, ability, and skill of others to bring clarity to our own lives.

I have since befriended a gentleman in his 50's, who through the death of his fiancée sought the help of a shaman in Costa Rica. A shaman as "(among certain tribal people) is a person who acts as intermediary between the natural and supernatural worlds, using magic to cure illness, foretell the future, control spiritual forces, etc." This gentleman needed to find relief from the depression that loss had caused. While he also had his doubts, he experienced significant benefits and relief from depression and anxiety.

There are people in this world who have God-given gifts for healing and helping people. If you believe in God, then you believe in the supernatural. Supernatural as adjective, means of, relating to, or being above or beyond what is natural, unexplainable by natural phenomena, abnormal. As noun, direct influence or action of a deity on earthly affairs. That day at the lodge, I had my own supernatural experience.

My mind and heart were now open to possibilities for total natural health, other than with prescription drugs and pills. After this experience, my transformation is clear. Oh how my life has changed! And, so can yours! Decision, patience and persistence are key. *Keep moving forward!*

I have let go of my past ghosts, demons, pains, and hurts. Now, when I go through the edit process for the book, the chapters containing the most difficult past transitions of pain, hurts, and emotional torment no longer have their same power or control. I have finally let go! When we make the decision to change and move on, you will attract and receive the support and help necessary for transformation.

"Neither do men put new wine into old bottles: else the bottles break, and the wine runneth out, and the bottles perish: but they put new wine into new bottles, and both are preserved." Matthew 9:17 – King James Bible.

Tested!

After several months of looking diligently for a new job without much success, I had resolved to the reality, that the corporate career doors were closing or had closed. I love to work, however I want to change from work to passion and calling. Many people love their work and working for a company or other entity, this is great! However, as we age there is a high probability that the choice to work for someone or something other than yourself, may be less and less. Then what do we do?

Accepting this reality was not difficult, I realized that other doors for life fulfillment were opening, and I was stepping into my new destiny. But wait! Sometimes, when we let go and move on, our decisions may be tested. In fact, expect to be tested. I received a request for interview from a major Telecommunications company. After sleeping on it, I accepted the request. The person conducting the phone interview was both passionate and persuasive for recruiting me for the position, and it was more of a conversation than interview.

After three decades of successful, corporate, professional experience, I expected no less, and I was delighted with her approach and respect. Midway through our discussion, while listening to the surf, birds and sounds of nature, I had a sense of peace, to wash over me like gentle cool waters. I had the thought, "I can't and won't do this anymore." The corporate stage of my life is over, and I have not looked back.

I walked away from a lucrative opportunity, at the height of my careers earnings potential, to be fulfilled from within - I chose passion and calling. I closed the door on seven-figure income. No more "golden handcuffs". I went with my heart because money is only one component of life, not everything.

Second destination Nicaragua: It's 9:00AM on a beautiful, sunshiny day, and I'm flying at 30,000 feet in a twin-engine aircraft, with the pilot, copilot, and 12 passengers in total. Looking out the window while flying from San Jose, Costa Rica to Managua, Nicaragua, I see two active volcanoes with clouds hovering above their peaks. I'm amazed at the photos my 4K camera is taking - such clear, deep, and vibrant colors, especially the blue pallet, the light, the dark, the blue turquoise and the blue-green..

The coral-blue color has become more and more present and getting more attention in my life over the past several months. Having spent several days in Panama, I now know why I had to take this trip. After many days of travelling and flying around, all of my senses are heightened, and I have total clarity. Why? Because I'm relaxed, at peace, and fully open to life and to the experiences and encounters the day brings. Feeling renewed and refreshed, heading to a new destination.

I can smell the combination of engine exhaust and fresh fruit for breakfast. Due to my heightened state of mind and consciousness, the usually sickening smell of engine exhaust, blended with other pleasant fragrances, made for a tolerable layered combo. I can touch the interior of the plane, the exit section just under the left wing. I can see the engine propeller through the lens of my camera.

I can clearly see the beautiful panorama below: Big, brown volcanoes protruding up with vibrant vegetation, small islands bestowed with shades of green flora and coastal beaches with varying hues of the beige, sandy coastline, and shades of blues for ocean water. I am even aware of my very breath, feeling *Completely Alive! Endless possibilities* await my acceptance.

Earlier, as I boarded the flight, I noticed two ladies who appeared to be in their 40's. One wore a scarf securely wrapped to her head, and her skin was an unhealthy, pale color. I took her hand to assist her aboard the aircraft. It seemed like she might have cancer, and the other woman, who I assumed was her sister, was assisting, and possibly caring for her. During the flight, the sister constantly rubbed and massaged her back to keep her warm. I don't know conclusively they were sisters; however, they looked very much alike, and their love for each other was so pure and family-bonded. In the span of the 75-minute flight, the joy, pain, and conscious awareness of my life had me in such an introspective and emotionally open place.

I've never been to Nicaragua before, but I knew I wanted to experience a new environment, culture, and destination, which aligned with my transition to my new life and awakened passions:

A.) To learn about other cultures and traditions
B.) To be open and free emotionally and spiritually to journeys that interest and inspire me, allowing me to engage, learn, and share
C.) To do the things I have always dreamed of, enriching my sense of the world and people, absorbing and sharing these insights

The transition to living my passions started with a decision to take charge of my life and take action to make my dreams and passions-reality. Others have done it, and so did I, and so can you. "Over 50" - it's easy to get caught in the trap of the "comfort zone", or as I refer to it "the casket of the living" - physically alive, but spiritually and emotionally devoid, waiting for life to steamroll over you, going through the daily motions without spark, energy, and passion.

After my last cry and letting go of past pain, hurt and imprint in Panama, Nicaragua proved to be the starting over point. We should look forward to, not fear, the unexpected - it gives us vigor! The unexpected takes us out of our comfort zone, provides armor and strength for changing, coping, and managing of life's transitions and challenges. Developing "attitude armor" is a life philosophy that creates strength, resilience, and comfort, that what even this "new" world throws at you, you are ready and able to handle it.

While writing portions of this book at a beach in Costa Rica, I observe children playing in the surf, no pretense of material things, simply indulging in camaraderie, and nature's bounty of surf and sand - lessons adults should heed. Across from the vast, majestic blue-green waters of the Pacific Ocean, lies a vibrant green jungle, a cacophony of sounds from monkeys, birds, and other fauna. My eyes are feasting on the pure and simple beauty to behold. My soul and mind are in sync, open, and content, reveling in God's creation.

When we open our hearts and minds to the journey of fulfillment and have faith everything will be alright, special and meaningful things start to happen. When seeking a better life and higher plane, our Creator, positive energy, and the universe align with us to position and guide our path for direction and reassurance. These are examples of people who took stock of their life and wanted more, wanted to wake up every day and be

excited about what the day will bring, and wanted to welcome the adventure, the experience, and the vibrancy of life lived as they chose.
1) The man who, now a widower in retirement, continued to pursue his dream of world travel
2) The engineer in Panama who became a beer master and lives on a small island with his family
3) The former photographer for a well-known nature publication is retired now, writing and living on a small Central America island
4) The flight attendant who is now retired, living on a small Central America island
5) IT sales professional who now owns hotels in Costa Rica
6) The retired secretary from Greece who travels the world with three suitcases as her only material possessions
7) The Dutch couple who are moving from Panama to Indonesia to manage a diving business and own no material possessions of any significant value

There is an awakening taking place in the boomer generation, an awareness there has to be more to life than raising a family, retiring, then planning to die, a desire for a life of contribution and purpose beyond societal norms. Being outside of one's comfort zone is definitely uncharted territory, and it can be scary, but it can bring vivacity to life, filled with fertile soil for new growth and fulfillment. I just needed to heed the call of the inner voice, which said I need to find my passion, change, and move on forward.

In my travels and journeys, I encounter and engage both single people and married couples "Over 50".

Here are a few of the common themes and situations I've found:

- Empty nest: The kids are on their own. What do we do now? And, are we still in love with each other?
- Divorce or loss of a spouse (widow or widower): How do I go on?
- Career or vocational transition
- Physical health challenges
- Children return to the nest ("boomeranging")
- Financial challenges or retirement: What to do now? Do I/we have

enough?
- Debt: Buying material things trying to fill the empty space within themselves
- Drug, tobacco, sex, &/or alcohol addictions
- Emotional and/or psychological health issues
- Loss of perspective and/or relevance
- Give up on dreams and/or passions
- Negative perspective

What are the "Top 5" common threads and reasons for these challenges "Over 50?"
1. Fear
2. Unresolved personal relationship issues
3. Reluctant to change
4. Life has depleted your ability to dream and move forward - it's easier to give up and live in the past than to create and live a different future
5. Loss of hope and relevance

Do any of these ring true for you? If so, what are you willing to do about it/them?

While traveling, observing, and listening to people "Over 50" who are living their dreams and passions, I've found they have one predominant thing in common: Their core group of family and friends are positive and share their dreams and passions. They either have an active, positive support network, or they live solitary lives and are very selective as to the people who they allow into their personal orbit.

People who make a decision to move out of their comfort zone are seekers. They are people who are comfortable being uncomfortable (or at least more comfortable than most) and who allow for natural growth and awareness with an adventurous, inspiring, independent, and out-of-the-box perspective.

I began my personal downsizing process at age 53 when I realized my material possessions owned me, instead of me owning them - the house, cars, furnishings, and clothes. I took inventory of my closets, clothes, and shoes, and estimated, over time, I spent more than $70K, and this was after

I had already given away lots of clothing to charities. That was a stunning revelation, and I was ashamed of my financial decisions, which were primarily driven by ego, image, and a partially empty soul.

It has taken over six years, but I've eliminated the $5K per month on mortgage and property tax, vehicles, furnishings, clothing and debt. I now live in a one-bedroom apartment with a bed, a chair, and a desk with several art pieces in process of being passed onto family and friends. Within the next four to 6 months, I will only own what I need. My expenses will be minimal, relegated to lodging, health insurance and food. That'll bring my overhead expenses down to less than one fifth of what they were.

I am developing land in Costa Rica and building a house there without incurring any additional debt. With pensions and investments allowing me to travel, I am living my passion and fulfilling my dreams - I am not rich or wealthy, simply meeting my needs in a modest and simple way. Americans, unlike many cultures in the world, seem to have a harder time downsizing and living with less. Maybe this is because we have so much, and our *wants* become more important than our (actual) *needs*.

Look for Light

Look for the good, and you will find it. Look for the negative, and you will find it as well. The positive seekers who I meet in life are searching for meaning and enlightenment. People seeking negative also find it, and they store it up, then project it out onto others. Positive people tend to have a brightly illuminated, multi-hued aura about them, and their positivity becomes contagious. It's easy to gravitate to them because their aura is like a lighthouse, beckoning you. Conversely, negative people seem to have a dark cloud, or dark aura, about them. They tend to want to add to their negativity circle; hence, the old adage, "misery loves company."

Mature people need to be surrounded by motivated, inspiring, positive, and passionate people to help navigate the challenges of a changing life. Throughout my life, I have attracted people and situations based upon my emotional and psychological state. When confused, I've attracted other confused people. When angry, I attracted angry people. When positive and happy, I attracted positive and happy people. It's the Law of Attraction in action, and it works every time.

Like a camel stores water, people tend to store emotional hurt, pain, stress, anger, and fear. Some even find comfort in their dysfunctions. Some are unaware of their issues. Therefore, they are not actively seeking solutions or healing; rather, they're existing in what they've become accustomed to. This is an unfortunate and sad state...and it doesn't have to be this way. They have suppressed their hopes, dreams, and passion not only from themselves but also the world as well.

For many baby boomers and seniors, suppression was the norm - it was expected and conforming. A life of suppression and expected conformity can lead to depression, aggravation, and frustration. This all takes you down the negative "path of prevention": *Preventing* you from being fulfilled, *preventing* you from being purposeful, *preventing* you from being your true self. For the "Over 50" crowd, it's time to reward yourself for all that you've done, all that you dealt with, and all that you sacrificed. It's time to make your life count for you!

I have lived days where I have felt disconnected from the world, as if the world was passing me by. Most of my friends are married, but I'm not in a relationship. I'm alone, and, while I am not lonely, this was not what I had imagined my life would be at 60. Though I had loving relationships with family and friends, something is still missing. Before the void or missing piece can be filled, I had to repair myself. I was living a partial life in the "living casket". My dreams and passions were suppressed, and I knew why. It was because of my past hurts, disappointments and insecurities.

My dreams and passions, as I approach age 60:

- Authenticity
- Health
- Living abroad
- Living my legacy, calling, and destiny

Authenticity:
To live and be me, intentionally me - without filter or social camouflage, living an authentic life is a dream of mine. All those years in Corporate America had created an artificial facade to never show or express my true and honest thoughts, suck up the injustices and harms with a smile, be a good "corporate citizen". I was sick and tired of this mask and the lies corporations indoctrinate into people. Go along and play the game, or fail. Wear one face during the work day and another in my personal life. This

mask no longer fits (if it ever did), and I made the decision to be myself (and no one else) full-time.

Maybe you feel the same way. If so, take off the mask, and move on from life's past box of pain, hurt and unfulfilled existence. Start living a life with enduring passion, full of anticipation.

Health:

I did not like the way I looked and felt concerning my physical appearance and the health conditions, which came from an unhealthy lifestyle: Tobacco, alcohol, unhealthy diet, and lack of exercise. My self-esteem was low, and I knew I was better than that. I knew I didn't get this way overnight and it would take more than a minute to turn things around in a positive direction.

Financial Freedom:

I wanted to create a personal brand and company that is authentically me, focused on leading, inspiring, guiding, and enhancing the lives of boomers, or "Over 50's". I wanted increased financial freedom to create generational wealth for my family and facilitate philanthropic giving.

Living Abroad:

I love Central America, especially Costa Rica. So, I purchased property in Costa Rica to develop for myself and my family for generations to come to live and enjoy.

Defining My Legacy, Calling, and Destiny:

I want to build my brand and company, having fun every minute of every hour of everyday, living life on my own terms. How? Through being of service to and for people, through books and articles and blogs, life coaching practices and outreach Programs specifically focused on life transitions, change, and transformation. As an advocate to inspire older people to live their dreams and passions in life's second half. To be an example of losing life's fire and passion, and regaining them "Over 50".

My legacy will live on through my relationships, memories, my deeds and how I've touched and transformed other people's lives. I am the architect of my legacy, and so are you! Share your wisdom, power and gifts. Keep moving forward. The world is waiting for YOU!!!

"Carve your name on hearts, not tombstones. A legacy is etched into the minds of others and the stories they share about you." - Shannon L. Alder

Decision and Change

At age 58, I made the decision to change my life; however, it wasn't a decision anchored in concrete. Why? Because I needed additional emotional and spiritual growth to solidify the foundation for real and sustainable change. I had to learn that sometimes we're just not ready for quantum leap change, and it takes a step-by-step approach, steeped in patience and understanding to fully let go.

From the time I made the decision to let go, seek answers, and be vulnerable, the voice on the inside was saying, "You are doing the right thing for you", "Keep going", "Burn your boat!", "Be your authentic self." "Burn your boat" is a phrase used to describe invaders, when they would raid a country - they would literally burn their boats, giving them no option for retreat. Once I made the decision to "burn my boat", my journey took less than two months. If I can do it, you can too, no matter your age, race, creed, color, socioeconomic status, country of origin, or any other "reason" you think you may have.

When you make the decision to change for a better, more complete, fulfilled life with passion, you can do it. Open your heart and mind to possibilities because your best days and years are ahead of you, not behind. Your dreams, passions, goals, and objectives can be realized.

In middle age, life can settle into complacency or "comfort zone", where little, if any, *real* comfort can be found. Why? Usually because of baggage from the past - we know something is amiss but may not know what or why or how to deal with it. Like the man who shared with me he only got married because he wanted a trophy wife, or the woman who told me she married her husband only for financial security, not love - we're stuck!

Remember, when we divert, postpone, or give up on our dreams, goals, objectives, and passions, it's like holding a beach ball under water. Over time, the ball gets bigger and bigger until it has to surface. The surge is coming. It's not a matter of *if*, but rather *when*. What will you do then?

I was once stuck in:

- Self-pity
- Ego
- Denial
- Anger
- The past
- Guilt
- Bad choices

Identify your "stuck" points, write them down, and take action. Over the past 10 years, with hundreds of conversations with people "Over 50", I have reached the following conclusions:

1.) Many men are driven by ego, based upon societal norms and expectations, which create:

- Narcissism
- Self-interest
- Self-intent
- Self-motivation
- Self-worth
- Control
- Power

2.) Some women are driven by security; however, when expectations of security are not met, then insecurity may take root and stunt or stop personal growth and development through:

- Indecision
- Poor judgment
- The past
- Low self-esteem
- Damaged personal relationships

Getting "unstuck" is the path to freedom, fulfillment, and purpose. There is a solution to every problem and situation - the choice is yours. What are your "stuck" point(s)? Write it (or them) down and take action in the 50-30-20 Day Plan Guide, available soon.

What I Learned:

Possibilities are only limited if I don't try. Vulnerability is the first checkpoint on the way to freedom. Take chances, do new things, and experience the thrill of the unknown. Our past can contain old and negative energies which block new and positive energies from taking root. Like weeds, emotional issues must be pulled out from their root, and, often, professional consultation is required to identify negative energies and deal with them at their source. Be open to experiencing the unseen, relax, and let it happen. Letting go of control is the ultimate control. Keep moving forward with positive expectations, no matter what the age.

Have a dream that's bigger than ourselves, define our unique destiny, and own it. Owning it means to take action, and keeping your passion fuse lit always!!! Enlightenment comes through discovery and explorations of people, things, and ideas. You are not alone. Pay attention to life's little affirmations. Leave nothing undone - purpose creates legacy. Life can be re-imagined.

Look forward to the unexpected; it gives us life! The unexpected takes us out of our comfort zone, provides armor and resilience for changing, coping, and managing life's transitions and challenges. Developing "attitude armor" is a life philosophy that creates strength, resilience and comfort, so that whatever this "new" world throws at you, you're ready and able to handle it. Create space and live outside your past BOX! Creating space means; creative thinking, to change perspective, or imagine beyond the box to a BIGGER LIFE!

"Stepping onto a brand-new path is difficult, but not more difficult than remaining in a situation, which is not nurturing to the whole woman."
- Maya Angelou

"Those who cannot change their minds cannot change anything."
- George Bernard Shaw

"Some changes look negative on the surface, but you will soon realize that space is being created in your life for something new to emerge."
- Eckhart Tolle

Notes and Affirmations:
_____
_____
_____
_____
_____
_____
_____
_____
_____
_____

Deanna's Journal
A Client's "God Story"

If you have ever been injured or cut that left a scar, then you know that eventually the pain goes away, and a scar forms over. Every once in awhile you may notice the scar and remember how it got there, but no physical pain. If you are still feeling emotional pain from your past, then perhaps the wound is still open and has not started the process of healing. Some things we will not totally get over to a point of 100% pain-free living. But over time, we should notice that the healing process is taking place and as each day passes the pain is not quite as bad. If you feel like the pain is not getting any better, but perhaps worse, than seek professional counsel. God allows seasons of sorrow and He is right there with us as we journey through them. But He is not the author of a lifetime of pain.

I'd like to share a story with you that illuminates some of the process, complete with pain-points, and hidden "signs" you will likely uncover when pursuing your passion. I pray this story resonates with you and something in it ignites a fire that could have only been lit by a source much greater than you. A flame designed and authored by a powerful and faithful God who loves you beyond comprehension!

I cannot tell you how many times God uses a client's story to provoke change and urgency in another client's situation. For me, giving credit and glory to God comes somewhat easy - because my only part in it is ensuring I ask Him to guide me. Prior to every client consultation, I ask God to please get Deanna out of the way. To only allow His thoughts in my mind and only His desires in my heart, and most importantly (for me and my mouth), is that only His words come from my lips to His beloved's ears. I am simply a willing vessel, that, when tuned to His station, can deliver messages and direction of His will to willing participants. I also have a responsibility to share His stories to inspire, motivate, encourage and direct others.

I have a very dear friend of over 18 years who loves to teach, and is a natural at delivering art lessons with astute imagination, passion, creativity, and fervor to children of all ages and adults of all seasons. We met while in telecommunication and technology sales.

Perhaps you have a co-worker who is just so much fun to be around that he/she makes the insufferable job you have actually bearable! She was that kind of colleague.

While sales was a lucrative opportunity, she longed to be in a classroom. Having a prominently "I" personality, she could (and often did) change jobs more than most other people. Rarely satisfied but for a small chunk of time, she always had her radar out for a better position. Sometimes, she would take a new job based on more income; sometimes, it was so she could sell the latest in technology, but always because she was unsettled at what it was she was doing for a living. She loved new adventures and thrived in ramp-up situations and learning new things. But, all the excitement of something new had a short shelf life.

The desire to change things frequently was inherent to her God-given personality, prominently an "I".

Finally, she made the brave departure from technology sales - brave because she was giving up stability, familiarity, and a high-end income. She initially bought a franchise that entertained children through art. She created a beautiful, safe, and abundantly-fun facility. Her pure, natural talent for decorating and transforming spaces into enchanting and inviting areas still amazes me. She had a knack for delivering God's many stories through art projects. She transformed the children's imagination and heightened their kinetic experience.

However, running her own business wasn't easy. Owning your own franchise and balancing parents' expectations with kids' positive experiences against profit and budget was no picnic. Still, she was living a dream...until, God communicated He had better plans for her.

Those "better plans" were not delivered on a silver platter, in neon colors, or with detailed written instructions (They never are!). They came through uncomfortable and untimely "changes" in franchise policies and procedures, rising facility costs, and newly-discovered insurance requirements. Changes that challenged her opportunity for financial success while also going against some of her core beliefs. God was asking her to take the next exit and trust Him. Literally, a step of faith. Of course, we only know that now, as we reflect back. At the time, it wasn't clear, only frustrating and depressing.

She eventually found her way to a traditional classroom. At first, she would tell you she had once again, "arrived at her dream job". She even was able to get back into leading an art class. I remember so well how excited she was to start that school year.

Well, unfortunately, the students were derived from one of two backgrounds: Either from one gang, or that gang's rival. Art class was an elective, and every student had to pick an elective. Band and sports, really any of the organized offerings, were not palatable to those students, so art class was the default option.

She was horrified at the thought some of her lessons included working with sharp tools. As it turned out, they had started carving paint brushes into borderline lethal weapons! Time for another exit, as orchestrated by a loving God. But, this time, she held on. Believing (as we all sometimes do), that this was what she was called to do. Even a little scared as the enemy allowed her to worry about the fact that her family needed the health benefits the school district was providing. They were great benefits. Her husband was working as a contract labor consultant and had been for many years. Stability in contract consultant was not the norm in the oil and gas business and benefits were not stable, if even offered at all.

Summer breaks came as a welcomed and timely oasis. Her "grace-tank" was surely depleted and a complete replenishment was absolutely necessary. It reminded me of how it was in Corporate America, where you were so overdue for a vacation that you would just "hold on" the best you could until the paid time off arrived. But, unfortunately, it took about four days to detox from the "stuff" you left, that by the time you started to relax and actually enjoy the vacation, it was over.

But, heading back for her third year, the pressure and discontentment came with another "sign": Health issues derived from stress. She went to the school nurse one day for scheduled health reviews. After taking her blood pressure, she departed the campus in an ambulance, having registered blood pressure of 283/140! She could have experienced a stroke, or, worse, even died! But, God had different plans and a much more powerful purpose for my good friend.

When removed from the toxic environment of the art classroom, her blood pressure became once again under control. Next, she made the change back to sales. Although, this time, she went for technology sales catered to educators and education facilities. She again was drawn to solution sales and delivered her presentations with enthusiasm and genuine value. She was always very good at sales.

Through what I believe was God's direction and allowance, she continued to experience change and chaos. Once again, finding unsettled feelings, deep down, that revealed her true purpose was not yet being utilized.

During this time, she had one son in college and her youngest finishing high school. Yet, it was time for a change. She and her husband decided to sell their home and head to the country. She was always a country girl. They moved onto some acreage, well outside of the suburbs, and built their dream home. Her purpose was coming into focus, clearer and clearer, one beautiful sunrise and sunset at a time. She invested in alpacas, which was to her husband a great investment, but to my friend, was a seed of soon-to-be unbridled love for these animals.

She was realizing her purpose, what brought her (and her husband) great joy and fulfillment. She still battled with holding on to traditional jobs vs. going all in (risk and all) with implementing the many ideas and dreams she was creatively designing.

She is currently a successful entrepreneur. Reveling and rejoicing in creativity and serving many communities through on-site and off-site animal therapy, a store, (and a store on wheels) featuring alpaca-fiber inspired products. And, best of all, she *still* offers art classes and summer camps.

She and her husband found a renewed passion for each other, as well as their farm. Realizing a dual-enthusiasm of combining love for alpacas and farm life (chickens, goats, llamas, and Great Pyrenees dogs), with unlimited, God-sourced sunsets! She is thriving and loving life! And, so can you! I'm so proud of her faith and living out her newly-realized, fully-ignited passion!

Here is the next layer of the story. As my friend was going through the health scare and recovery, I had a client who was attending my "48 Days to The Work You Love" class. She too was a teacher who was in dire circumstances! She was so stressed out, and so miserable in her job. She not only had students who were disrespectful, but an administration that added additional undue stress! Just sharing my friend's story gave her hope and encouragement to dream again and believe there are choices. Discovering you are not necessarily stuck in a job you hate just because you need the health benefits is a blessing in itself. But, in addition, you do not have to put up with an environment that is oppressive and stagnating in order to meet your income requirements and desired knowledge growth.

I'm happy to say, she too is doing much better and in a place where God is using her to bless others, as well as invest in a much more joy-filled, purpose-filled, passionate life.

We think we can dream big, but our Creator's dreams for us are SO. MUCH. BIGGER - guaranteed! He knows us better, and is much, much wiser. Most importantly, He comes with unlimited resources!

So, what about you? Where is your "sunset-inspired" epiphany? Aren't you tired? I was. She was. Max was. We still are, actually, but tired in a different sense. In a good way, like when you had a full day of doing what you have the most fun doing, balanced with healthy choices you feel good about, and getting to share it with your most favorite people in the world.

His timing is always perfect. Wait well.

CHAPTER TWELVE

From Caterpillar to Butterfly
Living It Every Day

"When it comes to staying young,
a mind-lift beats a face-lift any day." - Marty Bucella

10 Factors for Longevity and Ageless Life

From as far back as I can recall, my father's interest in physical prowess and nutritional supplements has been indoctrinated in me. He was a firm believer in the benefits of supplements in combination with exercise and a healthy diet. He would often experiment with various protein and mineral supplements to see if different combinations yielded better energy, stamina, and overall well-being. I attribute my initial openness and inquisitiveness to this early teaching. Over the years, I have expounded upon my initial understandings to include alternative medicine and nutrition and exercise from other cultures.

I developed a particular interest in Asian and Eastern India alternative medicine, nutrition, and exercise. Traditional Chinese Tao means "Way", or way of life, and is not a religion or deity. It also means "Path", which is the journey through life conforming to nature's own topography and time-tables.

One primary difference between Tao and Western ways is the Tao's attempt to connect man and nature while Western ways attempt to conquer (versus commune with) nature. I take an open-minded world view of everything both visible and invisible in life and the world. I have yet to find any belief, thought, or doctrine that 100% encompasses and conveys the totality of everything (except of course the Bible). This led me to be open-minded to the different practices and perspectives, particularly pertaining to health, nutrition, and medicine, as they relate to longevity and age.

The following ten factors for longevity and rejuvenation (ageing) are based upon a combination of Chinese Tao, Eastern Indian, and Western health practices, beliefs, and traditions. I have incorporated each in my personal health and wellness practices, and have, over time, reaped the many health benefits for preparing my Mind-Body-Spirit for potentially 40-plus more years of life and living. My focus is on quality of life, not merely surviving it. Maybe you feel the same way. If so, stay open-minded to all of life's options and possibilities.

*Blending Eastern and Western
Medicine, Nutrition and Wellness*

1. **Geography and Climate**

    In the 1980's, many studies of longevity have determined China is one of the world's top geographies for centenarians. Many live in remote mountainous regions, far away for urban and business centers with their polluted environments. Mountain-dwelling areas, with high dairy content diets, rank high in world longevity. The climate itself, with cooler and drier atmospheres, appear to benefit human health and wellness. We have many such climate areas and regions of the United States that fit this description.

2. **Diet and Nutrition**

    Diet is a primary contributor to healthy living, both in China and around the world. Chinese people, in particular, derive most of their calories from carbohydrates, vegetables, and beans in high-fiber, low-protein/fat, vegetable-based diets are all factors in longevity. Japanese, however, also consume a similar diet, but theirs is also based on raw fish (sushi), with an abundance of fresh vegetables and soybean-based products, unadulterated by cooking/heating.

Moderate daily doses of liquor or alcohol-based products may reduce the risk of heart attacks and stroke in the elderly. Notice: The key here is moderation. Since alcohol is a diuretic, avoiding consumption at night can minimize the number of bathroom visiting, and aid the sleep process. Water consumption, preferably purified, of *at least* 8 – 8 ounce glasses daily (64 oz), promotes food digestion and body hydration. I drink a 12-ounce glass of room temperature, purified water with lemon every morning as the first (fluid) intake of the day, then I eat breakfast. Drinking water throughout the day also gives me a sense of stomach fullness, which helps to minimize overeating.

The inside health game. Consistent daily elimination of waste products from the colons are critical to good health and longevity. Ideally, one should maintain the process of waste removal within 3-4 hours of each meal, resulting in 2-3 bowel movements per day. The human body thrives on proper nutritional intake, water, and timely elimination to prevent toxic build-up.

3. **Exercise and Breathing**

Healthy, older people, especially centenarians, incorporate physical exercise in their daily regimen. Yoga, Pilates, and breathing exercises are great for maintaining healthy and strong skeletal and muscle structures, which become more critical as we age.

The beginnings of yoga were developed by the Indus-Sarasvati civilization in Northern India over 5,000 years ago. The word "yoga" was first mentioned in the oldest sacred texts, the Rig Veda. The Vedas were a collection of texts containing songs, mantras and rituals to be used by Brahmans, the Vedic priests.

You can find several yoga and breathing video links for beginners, intermediate, and, yes, even advanced practitioners at our webpage: www.over50startingover.net - You can practice in the privacy of your home, until you're comfortable with practicing with others.

Yoga is my primary form of exercise. It is also a form of moving meditation and breathing that works for any age. It can provide the following benefits:

- Weight reduction
- Cardio and circulatory health
- Enhanced athletic performance
- Protection from injury

Lose the shoes, go barefoot as often as possible, connect with the earth.

The Art of Breathing

As the saying goes, "Control your breath, control your life." You can find practical breathing exercises on our webpage. www.over50startingover.net

4. **Environment and Stress**

It is critical to purify the bloodstream of pollutants from toxins in the digestive system. Excessive intake of alcohol, tobacco, fast food, and processed cuisines, as well as exposure to polluted air are all contributors to shorter life spans. Keep the colon clear and unclogged from toxic build-up and constipation. High-fiber diet and consistent water intake will result in healthy and unclogged digestive and colon tracts. There are several ways to improve indoor air quality, here are a few:

- Keep your floors fresh and clean
- Maintain healthy humidity levels; 30%-50%
- Maintain a tobacco-free environment
- Test for radon and asbestos
- Use natural, non-synthetic cleaners, such as vinegar for household cleaning

Nature and Healing:

There is no life quite like the natural life - harmony, serenity, and peace, in addition to human connection between natural elements, such as plants, trees, rain, water, sun light, air, sounds, energy, and animal life. We humans connect with many of these elements daily to sustain life itself.

We are products of our environment, which means it can *increase* or *decrease* stress, anxiety, and overall effects on well-being. Over the past few years, I have spent more time in nature than in the past 40 years combined. There is a stark contrast between my current health and well-being, and that of just 3 years ago.

I've embraced the connection between nature and my total being. I've increased my capacity for full daily and present environmental connection. I've included an early morning walk and jog on the beach or in the forest, daily meditation and prayer, healthy diet of fruits and vegetables, and rest. Many sources suggest (WebMD, Global Healing Center) that the color green may promote mood change, relaxation, reduced stress and anxiety, and provide restoration and rejuvenation.

Color is important for mental and psychological health and well-being. Evidence-Based Research (EBR) shows that color can impact healing and health processes. Colors vibrates in the trillions per second as it is processed by the brain. Our impact spectrum of light contains seven (visible) colors:

1. Red - Stimulation
2. Orange - Expression
3. Yellow - Optimism
4. Green -A "Master Color" - Healing
5. Blue - Serenity
6. Indigo - Meditation
7. Violet Indigo - Stress reduction

Feng Shui (pronounced "fung shway"), or "wind-water", is Chinese philosophical system of harmonizing everyone with the surrounding environment. Feng Shui concepts and design links are located at: www.over50startingover.net incorporates color as a key element that bind the universe, earth, and humanity together. Health care institutions use color as a primary element in interior and architecture design. Fill your living and work environments with colors that enhance your positive feelings, perceptions, mood is an easy way to better your life.

Stress

Three of the top-prescribed drugs in the US are for high blood pressure, or hypertension. Stress is a key contributor to high blood pressure and can be caused in many different ways: Daily job-related stress, traffic, or even taking a test. Some people get so stressed about speaking in front of a group, they'd rather have a tooth pulled. Short-term, or temporary, stress is normal and "baked into" the daily life processes and environment. However, long-term, or chronic, stress caused by events, circumstances, or situations that last for long periods of time can lead to serious health problems.

Problems that can cause chronic stress in midlife and senior years include, but are not limited to:

- Emotional problems, such as depression, anger, guilt, and self-esteem
- Physical issues, such as long-term illness, diabetes, heart disease, cancer, or prolonged pain and the like
- Transitional shifts, such as:
    - career change or job loss
    - divorce
    - empty nest
    - relational loss
    - loss of relevance
    - health
    - new relationships
    - retirement
- Family stresses, such as children, teen, aging parent or elderly relative with health challenges

Managing Stress

Identify who or what is causing you stress. Then, make adjustments and changes to cope, minimize, or even eliminate stressors. Here are a few things I do daily that have reduced the stressors in my life significantly over the past year:

1. Be proactive; don't wait until the last minute, make an appointment with yourself, put it on your electronic or manual calendar
2. Exercise daily to maintain a balanced stress-to-normal Mind-Body-Spirit equation
3. Eat healthy and minimize, or, better yet, eliminate, alcohol and tobacco
4. Get a good night's sleep of at least 8 hours. Alcohol is a diuretic, and when consumed late evening, can adversely impact sleep
5. Take the TV out of the bedroom; watching TV from the bed has a way of creating mental stress that can adversely impact sleep
6. Meditate, pray, or create alone time every day. I meditate morning and evening and pray several times daily. This can be as little as one minute to as long as one hour, or however you feel you need
7. Effective time management by avoiding overlapping, or back-to-back, schedules, especially when driving from Point A to Point B is required (and allow more time than you think you need to get somewhere in general)
8. Take regular time off for vacation or to just get away from routine, unwind, relax, and do as little as possible
9. Make a stress chart; for every stress, have a coping mechanism, even if it's calling a friend or enjoying a cup of coffee
10. Be assertive, and say NO! Don't try to please everyone or make everyone happy with you. It won't work anyway, so stop being a "pleaser"

> "Sex and golf are the two things you can enjoy even if you're not good at them." - Kevin Costner

5. Sex After 50

Do older people lose interest in sex after 50? Maybe, maybe not. Is sex still fun? Maybe, maybe not. After 50 the intimacy of sex may or may not be as consistent or satisfying as it use to be. Well it's not suppose to be. Older people after may seek a different kind of satisfaction and fulfillment. How about having fun with sex? And still achieving a level of intimacy and satisfaction, needed by both partners.

Sex after 50 for men and women should be needed and enjoyed. Healthy sex is combining Mind-Body-Spirit for complete and mutual partner satisfaction. In my younger years, I focused on more physical satisfaction through sex, than both emotional and spirit connection. In my 40's I began to understand the full satisfaction for sexual, thought, touch and sensual pleasures. Combined healthy Mind-Body-Spirit are prerequisite for a healthy complete sex life. I have learned through Taoist approach, and healthy lifestyle focus, to live and view sex as an integral part of the Mind-Body-Spirit equation.

Midlife and senior years can be a time to experience real intimacy that starts between the ears, not the loins. I won't delve into the societal and moral aspects of sex because my focus for this book is on other aspects. However, having said that, older people still have sex. (There is a great article on Huffington Post titled, "12 Things Everyone Should Know About Sex After 50", dated 04/13/2015.) Additionally you can find links about Taoist principles on sex at: www.over50startingover.net

6. **Passion**

For our purposes here, passion and passionate mean to be alive and vibrant with a positive outlook - this is the light within the human being, creating the fuel for achievement, bliss, and happiness. This feeling of enthusiasm and excitement is the fuel for achieving dreams. **Passion *always* WINS no matter your age.**

7. **Relationships**

Be your authentic self, and you will attract the right people to you. Healthy and positive relationships give us a sense of intimacy, belonging, caring, friendship, love, support, and self-worth. As we age, meaningful relationships are vital to passion, motivation, dreams, and vision. In middle age, the void or lack of relationships are fertile ground for boredom, loneliness, and depression. And this is a time of life where people are more likely to lose those much-needed relationships to death. Therefore, it is vitally important to remember: You are not alone!

There are so many ways to connect with people of all ages. Chapters 9 and 10 (Socialization and Life Team) provide practical means by which to connect with others, provides many societal and individual options for connection. And, check out our webpage for the "Over 50" community, where you'll find advice and support.

8. **Gratitude**

In today's world, no matter your age, it is very important to allow our body to find deep, restorative rest. Transcendental Meditation is the technique I use. It's an effortless technique that allows your mind to settle inward, beyond thinking, to experience pure awareness - the most silent and peaceful level of the mind, your innermost self.

Prayer for many people is a solemn request for help or expression of thanks addressed to God, a saint, or an object of worship. Prayer is the place of admitting our need, adopting humility, and claiming dependence upon a higher power beyond ourselves. For many, both meditation and prayer are connections to either one's inner self and/or supernatural energy or source.

For me, there's a difference between meditation and prayer. Prayer is a quiet connection with the Source and/or Creator (God), outside myself. Meditation is disconnecting from anxiety while still connecting to the harmony within. Nature's way of connecting life's dots for Mind-Body-Spirit.

The best things in life are free, especially nature. Spend a day in nature, walking, hiking, camping, water sports, or whatever you like, and compare the difference in sleep quality from being indoors in a controlled temperature (air conditioning or heat) environment to the splendor of nature.

The results for gratitude and thankfulness, is a smile and healthy sense of humor. A light hearted approach to life, is medicine for life's beach ball challenges within and without of our control. However you choose to do it, spend time each day in reflection and gratitude. You'll be profoundly healthier for it.

9. **Always Have a Dream**

Keep moving forward towards something special - if not for you, then for someone else. Thinking about others and doing for them are two of the most powerful passions and motivators in the universe. We have an imagination and creativity for a reason, to visualize and create.

In midlife, the gifts of imagination, creativity, and vision may diminish for many reasons. Boredom tends to be one of the primary culprits, especially in retirement. Recently, while visiting Costa Rica, I had a conversation with a couple of American ex-pats in their seventies. We were discussing the benefits of retirement in Costa Rica, and the 74-year-old woman (we'll call her Margaret) made the following statement, "Retirement is both heaven and hell!" The statement stuck in my head for several days. She described what so many retirees believe. Both she and the 76-year-old gentleman, John, cited boredom as the primary reason for "retirement hell".

In midlife, lack or loss of passion, imagination, creativity, and vision can result in boredom and inactivity. Having a dream *at any age* is the best way to prevent boredom from setting in, but dreams are crucial in our later years. Dreams are free and personal - boredom is dream-less and gets us STUCK. And, we now know STUCK SUCKS! Plus, one dream leads to another.

10. Vitality and Longevity - The Decision

I recently returned to the US from Costa Rica after a month-long stay, where I met a delightful young couple (about age 35 or so) from Hungary. We were discussing our separate, and mutual, motivations for visiting Costa Rica. I shared with them the status and process for writing this book.

When I stated the book's title ("Over 50, Starting Over"), the young lady asked my age. When I said, "I'm about to be 60", she said, "No way! You look to be in your mid-40's, no gray hair or wrinkles, and you have muscles everywhere. Can I see your passport?" I showed her my passport, and she said, "You look younger than your passport photo," which is now five years old.

This was such a compliment coming from people who I had just met. Funny thing is when I made the decision to create Mind-Body-Spirit health, looking younger and age reversal were not my objectives. I simply wanted to be, feel, and think healthier. You can be, feel, and think healthier as well - this can lead to longevity.

Since I changed my life more than a year ago and began to focus on total Mind-Body-Spirit health and well-being, people consistently tell me I seem to have reversed the ageing process - what a great feeling to be, feel, look, and think healthy again, especially after decades of physical, mental, and emotional neglect and distress! I've learned to attract what is good and positive into my life. I did it, and so can you!

Reinvention and age reversal are not only possible and attainable for anyone, regardless of age or life situation, it's also practical when you make *the decision* to live a life of fulfillment and meaning. Looking good starts with feeling good, and feeling good comes from a balanced Mind-Body-Spirit integration. Most people focus on one or two, usually their body, healthy diet, daily exercise, but still have little, or no, real purpose or meaning in their lives. Or, the reverse - they may have purpose and meaning, but with poor physical, psychological, or emotional health.

This is like sitting on a three-legged stool with one (or two) leg(s) shorter than the others. Make a point of integrating all three, and thus making sure all three are in balance and equal. Our website, www.over50startingover.net, contains a link to charts for natural herbs and vitamin supplements for:

- Stress and Pain Management
- Energy
- Sleep and Relaxation

Retirement:

At age 58, I left my corporate career behind, not to retire, but rather to step into my new and bigger life. Calling, purpose and meaning are now my life's motivations. My previous career was driven by work, money and fear, but now my life is driven by a labor of love to manifest a legacy of giving that will live on after I depart this life. There is no mention of retirement anywhere in the Bible. Retirement is a man-made idea and concept for financial support and resources beyond our "work" and "productive" years. Our second prime of life; or the *new* second prime is based on healthy Mind-Body-Spirit integration, for optimum living.

Now, living in both the United States and Costa Rica, and living my new life and calling, I have a deeper understanding of both the positive and negatives of the concept of retirement from the Expat's and tourists who I encounter daily: Don't retire and do nothing. Have a plan. Transition from one form of "work" to another. Make your passions your "work". Stay active always. Reinvent yourself, and create your life to meet your specific wants and needs.

Take risks, and try new things on a regular basis, be curious, and use your imagination. Again: Always, always, always have a dream - one dream leads to another. Create a clear and living legacy that will live on after you're gone (because you will be gone one day). Transition, passion and transformation, caterpillar to butterfly. Creating beauty through change.

In our next book, we will take a deeper dive into living life abroad.
Stay Inspired!

"Hope is not a strategy. It's positive anticipation and expectation."
- Max Gilreath

My beach ball issues at almost 60:

- Complete freedom
- Medication free
- Age reversal

The beach ball effect is where we suppress and ignore issues until they become real problems. While writing this book, I realized I had made many of my life's dreams a reality over the past few years; however, I'm still working on complete freedom and age reversal, bringing my physical body into a state of total health, freedom from prescription drugs. I'm free to do what I want when I want to do it, and I continue to build the "Over 50" brand with my business partner, and co-author, Deanna.

"Allow my pain to release you from yours."   - Max Gilreath

Don't Waste Your Pain

Like the musician and songwriter who found authenticity from singing and writing about his life's experiences, these many-years of life have led me to my place of calling. Perfect in my imperfections, grateful in both joy and pain. This is my life's song in the hope of inspiring you to find, and sing, yours.

I now have the full realization that every adversity, every pain, every happiness, and every joy that I've experienced was for a purpose. Deanna calls it "the sanctification process". This means to grow in divine grace as a result of (Christian) commitment.

Your sanctification is going through pain, enduring life lessons, learning and growing, knowing that there was/is a reason. You can't teach what you don't know. It could become your purpose as it has become mine. Everything, e-v-e-r-y-t-h-i-n-g, yes, I mean **everything**, happens for a reason (even if you don't know or understand what that reason is at the time). Everything has prepared and defined me, as it has you, for this time in life.

"Over 50" is an opportunity to define and live out your calling and, ultimately, legacy. Today, my Life Team relationships are strong and thriving as are my relationships with family, extended family, friends and associates. Global "Tribe" connections are growing and fulfilling. My Mind-Body-Spirit health and well-being are integral, and the best they've been in years. What the doctor prophesied over my life more than 50 years ago has come to pass: (Max has) "Something special to offer the world". How? In part, by writing this book, becoming a Life Coach, developing an outreach program, advocacy for older persons, and being of service for mankind. Filled with passion, meaning, and purpose, I'm truly living my calling. What's your calling? Find It! Live It!

Passion Always Wins

Deanna's Igniting Insights

A Client - Coach relationship evolves over time through battling the ups and downs of life's transitions. In the beginning of my collaboration with Max, he was reserved, cautious, and reluctant to my suggestions and proposed process. As he exposed his up-bringing, as well as life's experiences, it does not surprise us that he'd be resistant. In fact, throughout Max's story, we witness him having to figure out things about life on his own, with little or no explanation or guidance. Adults spoke "over him", not with him. He learned via what I call "lessons that are caught, not taught", leaving him to sift and decipher the good examples from those that were bad. And, when he faced events or situations that he had no previous reference to, he plowed through them by the seat of his pants, so to speak.

I'd like to use Max's example of how he responded to advice and direction to hopefully help you in discovering your path to lived-out passion and purpose. First, it took him awhile to reach out regarding career direction. He waited until his frustration grew to a level that impaired his ability to point toward wisdom and resolve. When life is coming at us like drinking water from a fire hose, we tend to delay the action we know we need to take. I encourage you to **take action *today***, on whatever it is you know you need to move forward from. Action starts with a decision. Decide today you will run fast and hard after what it is God has waiting for you. If it is you needing to reach out to a life coach, or faith advisor, or career transition expert, then make that call now.

Another lesson that can be derived from Max's story is to begin tapping into and confirming God's will for you. It's so easy for me to say, "You'll know when you know", but, really, you will. That dream deep inside of you will fester; then, when you ask your Creator and Author of life to implement the path that He has already provisioned, well, put your seatbelt on! You will get so excited about your dream that the Holy Spirit will wake you up at night thinking about it, and wake you up early in the morning, so you can do something about it! You'll. Just. Know.

Now, the confirmation of God's will, what it is exactly He created you for, that one may require help from others. First, pray about it, talking with

God about specifics, asking directly for confirmation. Ask others (those you trust who have faith and love for Jesus!) to pray for you in the same manner. Next, read His word. I hope you have experienced opening your Bible, to a random place perhaps, and having His words *jump* off the page and speak the very things you need to hear at the most opportune time! It has happened countless times for me and so many others I know. There are endless amounts of "God hugs" awaiting you in His word! Oh, and the divine advice - it gets no better than that! So, pick up and read His word.

Lastly, confirmation will come through the Holy Spirit. He will tug on you (lovingly), and engage in what I call a "full-court-press", occupying your every thought and stirring up your soul into actions of love.

When coaching, it is practically a guaranteed **home-run** when your client is one with his/her Creator. I truly do not know how these things called "life" and "life's transitions" can be processed and played out *without* the full knowledge of God's love and the depths of which He will go through to fully expose our purpose. But, you have to *ask* Him. He will transform a blurry dream into laser focus, under abundant magnification, for those who are willing to pursue Him and His will! When we claim to be His, trust that we are not called to be average or content.

When Max and I wrestled over challenges, choices, and decisions, it always pointed back to being one with God. In addition, the lack of movement forward was from a lack of belief in himself. When you get to this point, it is a test of faith. When you lack faith, you lack belief in yourself. ***Believing that you can obtain your dreams and goals is essential.***

As a coach, when you lack faith in yourself, I will exhibit enough faith in you (as my client) until I can illustrate and transfer wisdom derived from God's truth: You are worthy, and through God's confidence, you can move forward in faith and claim and live your purpose! The secret is, it really is just a faith test. When you lift up the layers of what I do, I help develop your faith until you arrive at a point of wisdom and knowledge that God is all you need. Our author of life (your life) wants to be in perfect step and stride with you, and with Him as our "exclusive life pilot" (Not a co-pilot, the ONLY pilot!), we cannot, and will not, lose! When we filtered the challenges of direction through God's word, prayer, and tuning into the Holy Spirit, the outcomes were as such that they could *only* be explained by God's intervention.

This entire book project, throughout every step in the process, there were many "God stories", so many, that at one point I told Max we will have to start a God journal. For example, every person who needed to be a part of this project: Editor, Publicists, Videographer, Cartoonist, Web-Designer, Web hosting company, Marketing experts, etc. All of these key relationships had *already* been established. We had met and already trusted those we needed to make this book come to life. The bonus is we have the blessed pleasure of working with people we already know and love - it's been a blast!

When you are in His will and following His purpose for you and your life, you will experience abundant joy and relevance that cannot be put into words. Your actions will reflect your heart's desire. The simplicity of what your life will evolve to be will begin to exhibit a peaceful spirit. One with renewed energy and excitement.

I want to leave you to ponder and breathe in these **truths**:

- You are worthy
- You are loved
- You are relevant
- You have much to offer
- You can do this

It's never too late!

I look forward to hearing your stories, what your God-breathed purpose is, and how the process worked for you to sort it all out and make it come alive. May you be inspired and filled with a renewed hope, armed with relentless faith, to live out your meaningful, purpose-filled, and passion-lived life!

Over 50 STARTING OVER ®

50-30-20 DAY PLAN GUIDE COMING SOON

Visit our blog for topics like:
Special Stories
Boomerang Kids
Taking Care of Elderly Parents

<u>www.over50startingover.net</u>
<u>www.interviewpreparedness.com</u>
<u>www.secondprime-coaching.com</u>

www.ingramcontent.com/pod-product-compliance
Lightning Source LLC
Chambersburg PA
CBHW081455040426
42446CB00016B/3244